REGGIO CALABRIA TRAVEL GUIDE

An Adventure to Explore the Hidden Gems, Must-See Top Attractions, Relaxation Hotspots, Culinary Delights, Insider Tips, and Unlock the Best-Kept Secrets.

FORTUNE N ARNOLD

Copyright © [2024] All Rights Reserved.

No part of this publication may be reproduced, distributed, or transmitted in any form or by any means, including photocopying, recording, or other electronic or mechanical methods, without the prior written permission of the publisher, except in the case of brief quotations embodied in critical reviews and certain other non-commercial uses permitted by copyright law.

Disclaimer

Please, note that the information contained within this document is for educational purposes only.

The information contained herein has been obtained from sources believed to be reliable at the time of publication.

The opinions expressed herein are subject to change without notice.

Readers acknowledge that the Author/ Publisher is not engaging in rendering legal, financial, or professional advice.

The Publisher/ Author specifically disclaims any liability from the use or application of the information contained herein or from the interpretation thereof.

Table of Contents

Table of Contents

Table of Contents 4

Introduction 10

    Why This Book? 13

    Unveil the Hidden Gems 13

    Explore Must-See Top Attractions. 13

    Indulge in Relaxation Hotspots. 14

    Savor Culinary Delights. 14

    Unlock the Best Kept Secrets. 15

Chapter 1: Welcome to Reggio Calabria 17

    Introduction to Reggio Calabria 17

    Location and Overview of Reggio Calabria 27

    History and Culture of Reggio Calabria 33

    What makes Reggio Calabria Unique as a Travel Destination? 39

Chapter 2: Getting to Reggio Calabria 45

    The Airports and Transportation to Reggio Calabria 45

Transportation for Getting Around in Reggio Calabria. 53

Nearby Cities and Transportation Links to Reggio Calabria 60

Chapter 3: Practical Information 65

The Best Time to Visit Reggio Calabria 65

Why Choose Reggio Calabria as Your Next Travel Destination 74

The Landmarks and Must-See Top attractions in Reggio Calabria 83

The Weather and Climate of Reggio Calabria 91

Chapter 4: Travel Tips and Resources to Reggio Calabria 96

The Visa Requirements and Entry Regulations to Reggio Calabria 96

Packing Essentials: What You Should Bring on Your Trip to Reggio Calabria 105

Health and Safety Tips for Travelers Visiting Reggio Calabria 113

Chapter 5: Planning the Perfect Journey to Reggio Calabria 120

How to plan a Budget-friendly journey to Reggio Calabria..120

How to Plan a Family-Friendly Vacation to Reggio Calabria...129

Chapter 6: Things to Do: Must-See Top Attractions in Reggio Calabria 138

Recommended Must-See Top Attraction in Reggio Calabria..138

Lungomare Falcomatà 138

Museo Archeologico Nazionale di Reggio Calabria ...140

Castello Aragonese 142

Arena dello Stretto 144

Museo Nazionale del Bergamotto 146

Roghudi Vecchio 148

Spiaggia Gallico Marina 150

Spiaggia di Riace 152

Spiaggia della Marinella 154

Spiaggia Di Scilla 156

Chapter 7: Exploring Reggio Calabria 158

    Historic Walking Areas in Reggio Calabria 158

    Cultural Tour in Reggio Calabria 160

    Archeological Tour in Reggio Calabria 162

    Boat Tour in Reggio Calabria 164

Chapter 8: Rest, Relaxation, and Accommodations in Reggio Calabria 166

    Tips and tricks of Getting the Best Hotels, Accommodation, and Vacation Rentals in Reggio Calabria 166

    Hotels in Reggio Calabria 174

    Luxury Hotels in Reggio Calabria 174

    Family-Friendly Hotels in Reggio Calabria 176

    Budget-friendly Hotels in Reggio Calabria 179

Chapter 9: Culinary Delights and Restaurants 182

    Foods and Culinary Delight that a Traveler or Tourist to Reggio Calabria Should Try 182

    Restaurants in Reggio Calabria 191

Chapter 10: Tips and Strategies for Having a Memorable Vacation to Reggio Calabria 195

Online and Offline Map Navigation in Reggio Calabria 205

On-line Maps. 205

Offline Maps. 208

GPS & Offline Navigation: 209

Basic Communication Words to help a Traveler to Reggio Calabria Communicate Easily........................211

Detailed Itinerary 216

A 14-day Itinerary for Reggio Calabria, Italy. 216

Conclusion 225

Appendix..227

Map of Reggio Calabria..227

Map of the Top Attractions in Reggio Calabria 228

Map of the Beaches in Reggio Calabria 229

Map of the Hotels in Reggio Calabria 230

Map of the Vacation Rentals in Reggio Calabria........231

Map of the Markets and Shopping Centers in Reggio Calabria 233

Introduction

The Reggio Calabria Travel Guide is your ultimate companion, packed with unique insights, expert guidance, and hidden gems to make your journey absolutely unforgettable.

Even if you're an experienced traveler or a first-time explorer, this guide will take you on a journey unlike any other.

Step into a world where ancient history meets breathtaking natural beauty, sun-kissed beaches combine with bustling city life, and locals welcome you like an old friend.

Reggio Calabria, located in the heart of southern Italy, is a treasure trove of delights awaiting discovery. And with this comprehensive guide at your disposal, you'll have all the tools you need to discover its hidden secrets.

What distinguishes our travel guide is its consistent dedication to provide you with a genuine and immersive experience. We travel beyond the conventional tourist attractions to reveal the hidden gems that only locals know.

Every page of this guide is packed with delights to discover, from the awe-inspiring beauty of the Riace Bronzes to ancient Greek statues that have weathered the test of time and the stunning landscapes of the Aspromonte National Park.

But it's more than simply the landscapes and attractions; it's the people, culture, and flavors that bring Reggio Calabria to life. Immerse yourself in the vibrant local customs, savor the delectable specialties of Calabrian food, and learn about the region's rich history at museums, festivals, and bright and colorful markets. You'll feel like a genuine insider as you navigate the busy streets with our expert guidance and recommendations.

Reggio Calabria is inviting you, and this travel guide will help you discover its treasures, deepen your awareness of its culture, and create unforgettable memories.

So, why wait?

Pack your bags, embrace the unexplored, and let the Reggio Calabria Travel Guide be your reliable guide on your wonderful vacation. This guide, with its tantalizing combination of spectacular sites, cultural marvels, gastronomic pleasures, and insider tips, is the key to unlocking this captivating region's best-kept secret.

Don't pass up the opportunity to explore the heart and spirit of Reggio Calabria. Your wonderful journey awaits!

Why This Book?

Unveil the Hidden Gems

Go off the usual path to find the hidden gems that makes Reggio Calabria really special. From friendly locals and breathtaking landscapes, you'll see a side of Reggio Calabria that few others get to see. Our efficiently selected itineraries will guide you to these hidden gems, allowing you to make experiences that last a lifetime.

Explore Must-See Top Attractions.

Exploring Reggio Calabria's must-see attractions will immerse you in the destination's rich culture and history. With our insider tips and detailed maps, you'll be able to easily tour these historic places, obtain a better appreciation of their significance, and immerse yourself in its timeless allure.

Indulge in Relaxation Hotspots.

In Reggio Calabria, relaxing takes on a whole new dimension. Even if you prefer the tranquility of a remote location or the pampering of an exotic spa, this guide will uncover the most exquisite relaxation locations for every discerning tourist.

Relax in stunning natural surroundings, revitalize your body and spirit, and let the stresses of everyday life go away. With our recommendations, you'll find the ideal place to rejuvenate and achieve inner peace.

Savor Culinary Delights.

Prepare to go on a culinary odyssey unlike any other.

Reggio Calabria culinary scene is a potpourri of tastes, combining traditional Italian food with contemporary flavors. You'll tickle your taste buds and stimulate your senses by indulging in traditional Italian foods brimming with local ingredients, as well as enjoying freshly made Italian cuisines.

Our guide will take you to the best restaurants, secret pubs, and colorful food markets, ensuring that each meal is a feast to remember.

Unlock the Best Kept Secrets.

We realize that true exploration is about discovering a destination's best-kept secrets. Our travel guide goes beyond the obvious, providing insider tips and local insights to enhance your Reggio Calabria vacation. From off-the-beaten-path hiking routes to secret spots with panoramic views, you'll be able to create your own one-of-a-kind journey and explore every possibility.

By choosing the "Reggio Calabria Travel Guide," you are not just getting a book; you are also accessing an experience that will broaden your idea of what travel should be.

This book does more than just show you where to go; it also introduces you to new ways to view, taste, and interact with your surroundings. Allow us to guide you on an immersive adventure, with each page leading to new discoveries.

The Reggio Calabria Travel Guide is more than simply a book; it is your key to discovering the wonders of this Italian paradise. With our experienced direction, you'll start on a voyage of discovery, immersed in Reggio Calabria's beauty, culture, and magic.

Even if you're a nature lover, a history buff, or a food lover, this guide will make your Reggio Calabria journey unforgettable.

Chapter 1: Welcome to Reggio Calabria

Introduction to Reggio Calabria

Welcome to Reggio Calabria, a fascinating city perched in the tip of Italy's boot. As you travel through this magical area, ready to be charmed by its rich history, magnificent scenery, and friendly residents. Reggio Calabria, or just Reggio as the locals like to call it, is a treasure mine of cultural legacy and natural beauty.

As soon as you step foot in Reggio Calabria, you will notice the dynamic energy that pervades the city. The air is filled with the seductive scent of freshly brewed espresso, which is a daily habit for the residents.

The city's streets are alive with the hustle and bustle of everyday life, with people congregating in bustling piazzas to converse animatedly and swap tales over steaming cups of coffee. The bright façade of houses covered with elaborate mosaics strike your attention, demonstrating Reggio's vibrant creative flair.

Reggio Calabria has a remarkable history that goes back thousands of years, and it proudly wears its old past on its sleeves. Founded by the Greeks in the eighth century BC, it has seen the rise and fall of countless civilizations, each with its own stamp on the city's identity.

As you explore the city, you'll come across vestiges of its old history at every step. The National Archaeological Museum of Reggio Calabria, located in an attractive nineteenth-century edifice, houses one of the world's best collections of ancient Greek art. The museum's crown jewels are the Riace Bronzes, two beautiful sculptures of Greek soldiers from the fifth century BC.

These marvels, precisely created and wonderfully kept, are a tribute to the city's rich cultural legacy, acting as a link between the past and the present.

Reggio Calabria is also endowed with natural treasures that will leave you speechless. The city is surrounded by the blue waters of the Ionian Sea, which creates a lovely background for its sandy beaches. Imagine wandering down the Lungomare Falcomatà, a magnificent promenade that runs along the shore and provides panoramic views of the sea and the Strait of Messina.

As you breathe in the soothing sea breeze and listen to the rhythmic sound of waves breaking on the coast, you will experience a profound sense of calm and peace sweep over you. The crystal-clear waters beg you to swim, while the welcoming beaches encourage you to relax in the warm Mediterranean sun.

The Aspromonte National Park, which stretches from the Tyrrhenian to the Ionian Sea, is a well-known sight in the city. This untamed sanctuary is ideal for nature lovers and explorers alike.

Lace up your hiking boots and set off on an exciting trek through the lush forests, breathtaking mountains, and tumbling waterfalls. The park supports a broad range of vegetation and wildlife, providing a look into the region's remarkable biodiversity.

From rare orchids and wildflowers to secretive wolves and golden eagles, Aspromonte National Park is a haven for nature to live undisturbed.

Aside from its historical landmarks and natural beauty, what truly distinguishes Reggio Calabria is its people. The residents, known as Reggini, are recognized for their kindness, hospitality, and enthusiasm for life. As you walk through the city's small streets, you'll be greeted with welcoming grins and genuine "buongiorno" from passerby.

Take a minute to talk to the residents, and you'll discover a strong feeling of camaraderie and pride in their city. They'll excitedly share stories about their traditions, customs, and local delicacies, and invite you to join the Reggini family.

Reggio Calabria is a culinary wonderland that will delight your taste senses. Indulge in the tastes of Calabrian cuisine, which is known for its simplicity and use of fresh, local ingredients. Enjoy foods like 'nduja, a spicy spreadable salami that lends a hot bite to every meal, and the famed "peperoncino," a chili pepper that infuses meals with taste.

Don't forget to accompany your dinner with a bottle of local wine, since Calabria is famous for its excellent vineyards that create strong reds and sharp whites.

As the sun sets over Reggio Calabria, spreading a golden glow across the city, you'll realize you've fallen under its spell. Whether you're exploring its historic ruins, bathing in the sun on its magnificent beaches, or simply enjoying the kindness of its people, Reggio Calabria will make an everlasting impression on your heart.

It's a city that encourages you to slow down, enjoy every minute, and immerse yourself in its distinct combination of history, nature, and culture.

So come and enjoy the delights of Reggio Calabria, where every nook has a story to tell and every encounter invites you to embrace the beauty of life in this intriguing Italian treasure.

Reggio Calabria invites you to explore further into its historical riches. Beyond the National Archaeological Museum, explore the city's historic core, where Roman and Byzantine architecture coexists with medieval beauty. Admire the Cathedral of Reggio Calabria, a magnificent example of Norman and Gothic architecture that reflects the city's religious tradition.

Lose yourself in the labyrinthine passageways, where hidden jewels such as the Church of San Giorgio and the

Church of San Francesco emerge, each with their own narrative to tell.

Immerse yourself in the thriving cultural environment of Reggio Calabria. The city welcomes the arts with open arms, sponsoring several festivals and events throughout the year. The Teatro Comunale, a beautiful opera venue, hosts a variety of exciting performances, including classical masterpieces and modern compositions. Explore art galleries that highlight the abilities of local artists, or go to a performance where the strains of traditional Calabrian music fill the air, creating a passion inside you.

Reggio Calabria's allure goes beyond the municipal borders. Explore the region's lovely seaside towns. Admire the colorful fishing towns of Scilla and Bova Marina, where time appears to stand still and the rhythm of life is determined by the ebb and flow of the sea.

Indulge in fresh seafood delights at quaint waterfront trattorias while enjoying Mediterranean tastes.

Further north, you'll find hidden jewels set among the harsh scenery of the Aspromonte Mountains. Explore beautiful mountain communities such as Gerace, which are set on a hilltop and decorated with antique churches and medieval buildings.

Take in the panoramic views of the surrounding countryside, where olive orchards and vineyards extend as far as the eye can see.

Reggio Calabria is a city that values its traditions and celebrates its heritage. Join in the Carnevale celebrations, where the streets are alive with brilliant parades, colorful costumes, and joyful music. Experience the excitement of religious processions honoring patron saints, and experience the Reggini's strong faith firsthand. Participate in the bustling street markets, where local craftsmen sell their wares and the scent of freshly baked goodies fills the air.

As your tour through Reggio Calabria draws to a conclusion, you'll have memories that last a lifetime. The city's rich history, magnificent scenery, and friendly residents have knitted themselves into the fabric of your identity.

You'll leave with a greater appreciation for life's basic joys, a revitalized sense of wonder, and a desire to return to this magical corner of Italy.

Reggio Calabria awaits you, eager to wrap you in its loving arms. Allow its allure and beauty to unfurl before your eyes as you embark on a trip that will make an unforgettable impression on your spirit. Discover the attractions of this enthralling city, where ancient history meets modern energy, and each step tells a different narrative.

Welcome to Reggio Calabria, where Italy's soul is brought to life via a symphony of sights, sounds, and feelings.

Location and Overview of Reggio Calabria

Welcome to Reggio Calabria, a captivating city located at the southernmost tip of Italy's stunning peninsula. With its rich history, breathtaking landscapes, and vibrant culture, Reggio Calabria provides an unforgettable experience for visitors looking to discover the allure of this remarkable destination.

Reggio Calabria, located in the Calabrian region, is surrounded by the magnificent beauty of the Ionian Sea. When you arrive at this coastal gem, you will be greeted by a picturesque setting where azure waters meet golden sandy beaches, and a gentle breeze carries the scent of citrus orchards dotting the landscape.

One of Reggio Calabria's main attractions is its magnificent waterfront promenade. This stunning stretch, known as the Lungomare Falcomatà, invites you to stroll along the azure shoreline at your leisure. As you wander, you'll be captivated by the panoramic views of the Strait of Messina, where the Italian mainland and Sicily almost meet.

The Lungomare Falcomatà is enhanced by palm trees, vibrant gardens, and elegant Art Nouveau buildings, adding to its enchanting allure.

Reggio Calabria is also home to the world-famous Riace Bronzes, a pair of ancient Greek statues from the fifth century BC. A scuba diver discovered these masterpieces in the waters of Riace in 1972, and they are now housed in the National Archaeological Museum of Reggio Calabria.

The museum itself is a treasure trove of artifacts that depict the region's rich history, which extends from prehistoric times to the Roman era. Admire the intricate pottery, exquisite jewelry, and captivating sculptures that provide insight into the ancient civilizations that once thrived in Calabria.

Immerse yourself in the city's historical center, known as the "Buzzacarini." As you meander through its narrow streets, you'll come across charming piazzas where locals meet to socialize and drink espresso.

Admire the Cathedral of Reggio Calabria, which combines Norman, Gothic, and Renaissance styles. The cathedral's majestic exterior and exquisite artwork within make it a real marvel. Visit the Church of San Giorgio, which is noted for its stunning 18th-century murals depicting Saint George's life.

Aspromonte National Park is a must-see for nature lovers. This huge wilderness, with its jagged mountain peaks and lush woods, provides a plenty of outdoor activities.

Lace up your hiking boots and explore gorgeous routes that meander through stunning landscapes, where you'll see flowing waterfalls, secret caverns, and a rich range of flora and animals. Keep a watch out for the elusive Calabrian wolf, which symbolizes the park's wild beauty.

Reggio Calabria is also known for its wonderful food, which incorporates the freshest local products and tastes. Indulge in classic Calabrian cuisine like 'nduja, a spicy spreadable salami, or enjoy the simplicity of handmade pasta with locally obtained olive oil and juicy tomatoes.

Don't forget to try the region's renowned citrus fruits, notably the famed bergamot, which is used to make aromatic essential oils. Enjoy the rich tastes of Calabrian chili peppers, which provide a fiery bite to many regional cuisine.

Reggio Calabria is busy with festivals and cultural activities all year long. Experience the exciting ambiance of the Festa della Madonna, a religious event held in September when the city is decked out in bright colors and processions flood the streets.

Immerse yourself in the joyful beats of the Tarantella, a traditional dance performed at numerous celebrations when both residents and visitors participate in the lively revelry.

As you visit Reggio Calabria, you'll discover a city that seamlessly combines history, natural beauty, and kind friendliness. Its warm and friendly attitude, mixed with the breathtaking scenery, will make an everlasting impression on your heart and spirit.

Reggio Calabria is a place that promises to meet your every desire, whether you want to relax on the beach, travel through historical civilizations, or go on an adventure in the vast outdoors.

So pack your bags and let the charm of Reggio Calabria carry you to a world where history, culture, and natural beauties combine to create an experience unlike any other.

From the beautiful waterfront promenade to the ancient treasures of the Riace Bronzes, this coastal jewel will provide you with memories that last a lifetime.

Prepare to be enchanted by Reggio Calabria's seductive appeal and immersed in the beauty of this Italian seaside paradise.

History and Culture of Reggio Calabria

Reggio Calabria, Italy: A Journey of History and Culture

Welcome to Reggio Calabria, located at the toe of Italy's boot. As you walk through its bustling streets, you'll be enthralled by the rich history and culture that pervade every nook.

Let us go on a journey through time to discover the intriguing history of this historic city.

Reggio Calabria has a millennia-long history, having origins in ancient Greece. The Greeks established the city in the eighth century BCE, and it was originally called as Rhegion. Its strategic location on the Strait of Messina made it a major trading and business center in the Mediterranean. As you explore its archeological riches, you'll come across traces of the beautiful past.

The National Archaeological Museum of Reggio Calabria includes one of the world's most well-known collections of Greek sculptures, including the famed Riace Bronzes.

These intriguing sculptures, unearthed in the 1970s off the shore of Riace, show two great warriors and serve as a tribute to the city's classical legacy.

Marvel at the delicate intricacies of these bronze sculptures, dating back to the 5th century BCE, and envision the talented hands that created them.

The city's architecture and cultural traditions continue to reflect the impact of Greek culture. As you walk through the streets, you will notice Greek-inspired columns, arches, and frescoes on numerous buildings.

The Teatro Comunale, a stunning opera house built in the late nineteenth century, with a neoclassical architecture evocative of ancient Greek theaters and provides an amazing cultural experience. Attend a show and let the beautiful music and stunning performers to transport you to another world.

Reggio Calabria is not only a city of ancient treasures, but also a gateway to the natural splendor of the Calabrian peninsula. Nestled between the glittering seas of the Ionian and Tyrrhenian Seas, the city provides spectacular views of the coastline and the majestic Mount Etna in nearby Sicily. T

ake a leisurely stroll along the picturesque Lungomare Falcomatà, Europe's longest coastal promenade, and be captivated by the turquoise water and pleasant air. Gaze out at the horizon, where the sky and water merge into a colorful tapestry, and you will experience inner peace.

The city's culture is firmly anchored in its close-knit community and love of art and music. Reggio Calabria is well-known for its traditional folk music, which resonates through the streets during festivals and festivities.

 The tarantella, a frenetic dance accompanied by the rhythmic sounds of tambourines and accordions, will urge you to join in the fun and feel the residents' dynamic enthusiasm. Lose yourself in the festive mood as music and dance fill the air, and let the beat sweep you away.

To completely immerse yourself in the local culture, taste Reggio Calabria's gastronomic offerings. The region's food celebrates fresh, locally sourced products and traditional traditions passed down through generations.

Enjoy the tastes of foods such as 'nduja, a spicy and spreadable salami, or the legendary "pasta alla Norma," a delightful pasta dish named after the opera by local composer Vincenzo Bellini. Pair your dinner with a glass of Ciro, a well-known local wine, and enjoy the symphony of flavors.

Reggio Calabria is a city that values its religious history. The towering Cathedral of Maria Santissima Assunta, with its spectacular Byzantine and Norman architecture, exemplifies the city's religious devotion. Step inside the cathedral and be amazed by its magnificent mosaics and rich embellishments, which convey stories of faith and devotion.

As sunlight flows through the stained glass windows, producing a kaleidoscope of hues, you can't help but feel reverent and peaceful.

As you say goodbye to this enthralling city, take a minute to think on the history and culture you've experienced.

Reggio Calabria, with its historic origins, vibrant traditions, and breathtaking beauty, leaves an unforgettable impression on the hearts of those who visit. If you're drawn to its ancient riches, natural beauty, or rich culinary legacy, this city will provide a fascinating trip through time and culture.

In Reggio Calabria, you've discovered a location where history lives on, where echoes of the past blend with the vivid pulse of the present.

 Accept the warmth of its people, immerse yourself in its charming streets, and let the essence of this extraordinary city to make an indelible effect on your soul.

What makes Reggio Calabria Unique as a Travel Destination?

Discover the charming city of Reggio Calabria, a hidden jewel in southern Italy. As you go to this enchanting place, you will be charmed by Reggio Calabria's distinct charm and unsurpassed beauty. With its rich history, magnificent scenery, and vibrant culture, Reggio Calabria is a genuinely unique tourism destination.

One of the most striking features of Reggio Calabria is its breathtaking natural beauty. Consider wandering along the scenic Lungomare Falcomatà, a promenade that runs along the dazzling shore. As you breathe in the fresh sea air, you'll be captivated by the panoramic views of the stunning Strait of Messina and the rugged mountains that surround the city.

The crystal-clear waves of the Ionian Sea invite you to put your toes in and enjoy the calm of the surroundings.

Reggio Calabria is also home to one of Italy's most valuable treasures, the Riace Bronzes. These magnificent ancient statues, dating from the fifth century BC, were discovered in the waters around Riace and are now housed in the National Archaeological Museum of Reggio Calabria.

Standing in front of these majestic masterpieces, you'll feel a deep connection to the past and awe at the ancient world's artistic genius.

The city's historical significance is just as compelling. Reggio Calabria has a rich heritage dating back thousands of years, and its strategic location has made it a crossroads for civilizations throughout history. As you wander the small alleyways of the historic district, you'll come across vestiges of ancient Greek, Roman, and Byzantine civilizations. Immerse yourself in the lively ambiance of Piazza Italia, the city's main plaza, where you can appreciate the neoclassical architecture while sipping a delicious espresso at one of the lovely cafés.

Reggio Calabria's cultural landscape is booming, providing a lovely mix of classic and contemporary activities. The city is well-known for its vivid festivals and events, which highlight its distinct traditions and customs.

During the Festa della Madonna della Consolazione, the streets are filled with processions, music, and vibrant parades. As you join the locals in celebrating, you'll experience a sense of belonging and gratitude for the warmth and kindness of the Reggio Calabrians.

Reggio Calabria offers a gourmet excursion with authentic Calabrian delicacies. Enjoy recipes brimming with the rich tastes of sun-ripened tomatoes, locally produced olive oil, and fragrant herbs. Try regional delights like 'nduja, a spicy spreadable salami, and the famed bergamot fruit, which is endemic to the region and provides a distinct flavor to pastries and liqueurs.

Local markets are a sensory feast, with a variety of fresh fruit, cheeses, and seafood to satisfy even the most sophisticated foodie.

Reggio Calabria's closeness to the breathtaking Aspromonte National Park is a nature lover's dream. Escape the hustle and bustle of the city and explore the harsh countryside, where you may stroll through deep woods, uncover secret waterfalls, and breathe in the refreshing mountain air.

The park also has uncommon flora and animals, such as the stately Calabrian fir and the elusive Apennine wolf. Immerse yourself in nature's peace, allowing the beauty of your surroundings to refresh your spirit.

What genuinely distinguishes Reggio Calabria as a tourism destination is its unique and pristine nature. Unlike other of Italy's more well-known tourist destinations, Reggio Calabria has managed to retain its authentic appeal while being relatively unknown to the general public.

Here, you may discover the authentic flavor of Italian life by mixing with residents eager to share their tales and customs.

Reggio Calabria provides an exciting and wonderful vacation experience. From its magnificent scenery and historical treasures to its vibrant culture and kind friendliness, this city has a certain attraction that will captivate your heart.

Even if you visit its ancient buildings, indulge in its gastronomic pleasures, or immerse yourself in its natural marvels, Reggio Calabria will make an unforgettable impression on your spirit.

So pack your luggage, start on this incredible journey, and let the enchantment of Reggio Calabria sweep you off your feet.

Chapter 2: Getting to Reggio Calabria

The Airports and Transportation to Reggio Calabria

Welcome to your vacation to Reggio Calabria, Italy! In this detailed guide, we will look at the airports and transportation choices available to guarantee a smooth and comfortable journey.

From the minute you arrive in Italy to your final destination, we will provide you with all of the information you need to navigate the airports and transportation systems like a native.

Arriving at Reggio Calabria.

Your adventure begins as you land at Reggio Calabria Airport, commonly known as Aeroporto dello Stretto. Located just 5 kilometers south of the city center, this modern and well-connected airport welcomes visitors from all over the world.

The airport provides a variety of conveniences, such as currency exchange, vehicle rental services, and food options, ensuring that you have all you need upon arrival.

Transportation from the Airport

After you've collected your bags, you'll have numerous simple transit alternatives to go to the center of Reggio Calabria. Taxis are readily available right outside the terminal, providing a convenient and direct route to your destination.

The cheerful drivers will help you with your luggage and give a comfortable ride to your hotel or any other chosen place in the city.

Alternatively, you may take advantage of the local bus services, which are a low-cost choice for budget-conscious tourists. The bus station is conveniently positioned near the airport exit, and the routes serve numerous parts of Reggio Calabria.

The bus system is dependable, and the rates are reasonable, making it a good alternative for people want to experience the local method of getting around.

If you want to travel independently, automobile rentals are available at the airport. Numerous trustworthy rental businesses provide a diverse range of cars to meet your needs, allowing you to explore the breathtaking Calabrian scenery at your leisure. You may hire a car in advance or upon arrival, and rental desks are available in the arrivals area.

With a car, you will explore not just the city's attractions, but also the nearby towns, villages, and scenic coastlines.

Exploring the city.

Reggio Calabria has an efficient and well-organized transit system, which makes it simple to traverse and explore the city. AMT operates local buses that cover a variety of routes around Reggio Calabria and its vicinity.

Buses, with their regular schedules and low rates, are a good method to explore major destinations like the National Archaeological Museum of Magna Graecia and the lovely promenade, Lungomare Falcomatà. Tickets can be purchased directly from the driver or at approved kiosks.

Consider having a leisurely stroll through the city center. Reggio Calabria is a small city, with many of its key attractions, attractive piazzas, and local restaurants within walking distance. You may meander through the small alleyways, take in the colorful ambiance, and find hidden jewels along the way.

If you want to travel farther afield, the train network provides great links to other cities in Calabria and outside. The primary rail station, Reggio di Calabria Centrale, is conveniently located in the city center and offers frequent service to famous locations like as Catanzaro, Lamezia Terme, and Naples.

The trains are pleasant, dependable, and provide beautiful views of the Calabrian countryside as you journey to your destination.

Discovering the Region.

While Reggio Calabria is a wonderful location, the region has a plethora of natural beauty and historical places to discover. To completely immerse oneself in the Calabrian experience, hiring a car is strongly advised. With your own wheels, you can explore the breathtaking Aspromonte National Park, which has scenic landscapes, hiking routes, and quaint villages. The park is a nature lover's heaven, with chances for hiking, mountain biking, and animal watching.

You may explore the steep highlands, visit small mountain communities such as Gambarie, and take in spectacular panoramic landscapes.

For a beach getaway, visit the adjacent village of Scilla, which is noted for its lovely seaside appeal and the legendary sea monster Scylla from Homer's Odyssey. The trip down the coast is a picturesque joy, with stunning vistas of the blue Tyrrhenian Sea. In Scilla, you may relax on the sandy beaches, see the picturesque fishing hamlet, and eat delicious seafood at waterfront restaurants.

The Strait of Messina offers the possibility for an unforgettable day excursion. A ferry to Messina, Sicily, may be taken from Villa San Giovanni, which is only a short drive from Reggio Calabria. This short excursion rewards you with breathtaking views of the strait and allows you to experience the distinct cultural blend that exists between the Italian mainland and the island of Sicily.

Messina's historical features include the Messina Cathedral and the famous astronomical clock in the Piazza del Duomo.

Reggio Calabria welcomes you with open arms and provides a flawless travel experience from the time you arrive at the airport. Exploring the city and surrounding areas is simple and convenient thanks to a variety of transportation options including as taxis, buses, and vehicle rentals.

Even if you're drawn to the city's history, the breathtaking natural scenery, or the delectable local food, Reggio Calabria guarantees a memorable experience that will leave you with lasting memories. Accept the beauty of this southern Italian treasure and let the transportation alternatives lead you to unforgettable adventures.

Your journey to Reggio Calabria begins at the airport and continues through the city's attractions and beyond.

Transportation for Getting Around in Reggio Calabria.

When you visit the lovely city of Reggio Calabria, Italy, you will be pleased to learn that there are several transportation alternatives available to assist you explore and navigate the city with ease.

Reggio Calabria has a variety of transportation options, from traditional to modern, to meet your interests and needs.

Let's start with the most common mode of transportation in the city: walking. Reggio Calabria is a pedestrian-friendly city, and walking through its picturesque streets is an unforgettable experience. As you go about, you'll be drawn to the ancient buildings, colorful marketplaces, and friendly inhabitants.

Take your time to absorb the distinct ambiance and find hidden jewels around every turn. Walking allows you to fully immerse yourself in the city's rich culture and experience its genuine charm.

Explore the lively Corso Garibaldi, the city's main thoroughfare dotted with stores, cafés, and restaurants. Don't miss the Piazza Italia, a vibrant square where you can unwind and people-watch.

If you prefer a speedier means of transportation, the local bus system is a fantastic option. The buses in Reggio Calabria are well-maintained, dependable, and affordable. The large network of bus lines connects the whole city, making it easy to get to practically any place.

The buses are outfitted with comfortable seats and air conditioning, offering a pleasant ride even during the hot summer months. The bus drivers are polite and helpful, so don't be afraid to ask for directions or recommendations for the finest spots to visit. Tickets may be purchased at specified kiosks or straight from the driver as you board the bus.

Cycling is a prominent mode of transportation in Reggio Calabria. The city has developed a bicycle-sharing scheme, which allows you to borrow a bike and explore at your leisure. Pedaling around the city streets offers a new viewpoint, allowing you to find hidden lanes and gorgeous parks that might otherwise go unnoticed.

Cycling is not only an environmentally responsible mode of transportation, but it also allows you to interact with the local people and gain a more personal understanding of the city. You may ride along the Lungomare Falcomatà, a picturesque waterfront promenade with panoramic views of the Strait of Messina and the Sicilian coast.

Taxis are widely accessible around Reggio Calabria for anyone seeking a more private and convenient mode of transportation. Taxis provide door-to-door service, allowing you to arrive at your destination directly and without fuss. Taxi drivers are educated about the city and can give useful information and recommendations.

Taxis can get you to the beach, the National Archaeological Museum, or the lively Corso Garibaldi quickly and efficiently. You can easily find cabs at approved taxi stands or hail one on the street. Before you begin your travel, remember to check the meter and make sure it is switched on.

If you want to travel further and see the nearby areas, renting a car is an excellent choice. Reggio Calabria offers various car rental firms that offer a diverse range of automobiles to meet your needs. Having a car allows you to create your own schedule and explore neighboring sights like the famed Riace Bronzes and the scenic Aspromonte National Park. However, bear in mind that traffic in the city may be congested, especially during peak hours, so plan your routes and leave additional time for your excursions. Parking places may be restricted in some regions, so acquaint yourself with the parking restrictions and hunt for authorized parking lots.

Ferries and boats are available at the Reggio Calabria port for visitors interested in exploring the picturesque coastline and adjacent islands. These nautical choices offer an appealing opportunity to enjoy the stunning views of the crystal-clear waters while also immersing yourself in the region's coastline splendor.

If you're planning a day trip to Sicily or simply want to take a relaxing boat ride along the coast, ferry services provide a unique experience. You may take a ferry to Messina, a thriving city in Sicily, to discover its ancient attractions and wonderful food.

It is essential that you verify ferry timetables ahead of time, since they may change depending on the season.

Reggio Calabria also has a small airport, Aeroporto dello Stretto, which operates both local and international flights. If you prefer to go by air, the airport offers easy access to major Italian towns and other European locations.

The city core is easily accessible from the airport via taxi or public transit. The airport also provides automobile rental services, allowing you to have a vehicle available as soon as you arrive.

Reggio Calabria provides a diverse range of transportation options to enhance your experience of exploring this enchanting city.

Even if you choose to walk and embrace the local ambiance, take advantage of the efficient bus system, cycle through the streets, or opt for the convenience of taxis or car rentals, navigating Reggio Calabria will be a seamless and enjoyable endeavor. So, pack your curiosity, board your preferred form of transportation, and start on an unforgettable tour through the bustling streets of Reggio Calabria.

As you explore the wonderful city of Reggio Calabria, immerse yourself in its rich history, savor its gastronomic pleasures, and make unforgettable memories.

Nearby Cities and Transportation Links to Reggio Calabria

When you visit the beautiful province of Reggio Calabria in Italy, you'll be happy to discover a plethora of adjacent cities to explore. These cities, with their rich history and cultural legacy, are conveniently accessible via a well-connected transit network, ensuring a smooth experience as you begin on your voyage of discovery.

Messina, located just over the Strait of Messina, is a nearby city worth visiting. This bustling city is easily accessible by a short boat journey from Reggio Calabria's harbor. As you cruise across the crystal-clear seas, you'll be treated to stunning views of the coastline, with Mount Etna looming in the background.

When you arrive in Messina, you will be attracted by its attractive ambiance, which is defined by its gorgeous architecture and bustling streets. Don't miss the chance to see the Cathedral of Messina, a remarkable monument that combines several architectural styles, including Norman and Baroque.

If you want to experience ancient history, a visit to Catania is a necessity. It is advantageously placed on Sicily's eastern coast, and can be readily reached by train from Reggio Calabria. Catania has a rich history reaching back to ancient times, and you'll be immersed in it as you visit the well-preserved ruins and archeological sites.

The city is overshadowed by Mount Etna, Europe's most active volcano, which provides an awe-inspiring background for your travels. Take a stroll around Catania's lively streets, enjoy local foods at the busy fish market, and see the historic Teatro Massimo Bellini, a magnificent opera theater that hosts spectacular performances.

Consider visiting the charming city of Cosenza, located in the midst of the Calabrian countryside. Cosenza is easily accessible by train from Reggio Calabria, and the ride is picturesque, passing through rolling hills and green surroundings.

When you arrive in Cosenza, you'll be enchanted by its well-preserved old town, which features small cobblestone alleyways and exquisite medieval architecture.

Don't miss the chance to see the majestic Cosenza Cathedral, a superb example of Norman architecture, and the Rendano Theater, a cultural jewel that offers a range of creative acts throughout the year.

If you're looking for a seaside getaway, Tropea entices with its beautiful beaches and gorgeous vistas of the Tyrrhenian Sea. Tropea, located along the gorgeous Coast of the Gods, is readily accessible from Reggio Calabria either rail or vehicle.

When you arrive in this coastal paradise, you'll be met with golden sand beaches, turquoise waters, and a picturesque medieval center built on a cliff above the sea.

Take a stroll down the promenade, eat great seafood at the local trattorias, and soak up the sun on the lovely beaches that have earned Tropea the nickname "Pearl of the Tyrrhenian Sea."

Transportation links in Reggio Calabria are substantially established, allowing for easy and convenient travel to these surrounding cities. Tito Minniti Airport, the city's international airport, provides local and international flights to major cities in Italy and elsewhere.

The major railway station, Reggio di Calabria Centrale, offers regular train connections to a variety of locations, allowing you to conveniently visit not just local cities but also the rest of Italy.

An efficient ferry service connects Reggio Calabria and Sicily, providing a handy mode of transit to towns like as Messina and Catania. The boats are comfortable and provide breathtaking views of the surrounding scenery, making the ride an unforgettable experience.

When you arrive in Reggio Calabria, you will be pleasantly surprised by the number of adjacent cities waiting to be explored.

Even if you choose to see the historic wonders of Messina and Catania, immerse yourself in the charm of Cosenza, or rest on the beaches of Tropea, you'll be spoilt for choice. With an outstanding transportation network at your disposal, your travel from Reggio Calabria to these surrounding cities will be smooth, allowing you to make unforgettable experiences while exploring southern Italy's cultural richness.

Chapter 3: Practical Information

The Best Time to Visit Reggio Calabria

Welcome to Reggio Calabria, a beautiful seaside city located in southern Italy. As you plan your trip to this lovely region, consider the optimal time to completely enjoy everything Reggio Calabria has to offer. The city has a rich history, beautiful scenery, and a thriving culture.

Reggio Calabria offers something for everyone, even you enjoy history, the seaside, or traditional Italian food.

Read on to discover the best time to visit this charming city and make the most of your vacation.

Springtime Magic

Reggio Calabria actually comes alive in the spring, making it a great time to visit the city. From March to May, the weather is nice, with typical temperatures ranging from 15 to 20 degrees Celsius (59 to 68 degrees Fahrenheit).

The region's lush foliage is in full bloom, and bright flowers adorn the landscapes, providing a magnificent backdrop for your activities.

During the spring, you may visit historical places such as the Aragonese Castle, a magnificent castle that overlooks the city, and the National Archaeological Museum, which holds an astonishing collection of ancient relics.

Take leisurely strolls along the Lungomare Falcomatà, the city's coastal promenade, and enjoy the splendor of the glittering Ionian sea. The sunny skies and pleasant temperatures make it ideal for seeing the neighboring Riace Bronzes, which are iconic ancient Greek figures that must be seen.

This is an excellent time to sample traditional Calabrian meals at local restaurants, as the city conducts a number of food festivals honoring its culinary delicacies. Taste the tastes of the area with meals like 'nduja, a spicy spreadable salami, and try the well-known Calabrian wines, which go nicely with the local food. Spring provides an excellent blend of nice weather, cultural events, and gastronomic pleasures.

Summer Bliss.

If you enjoy the sun, Reggio Calabria thrives throughout the summer months. Temperatures spike between June and August, reaching 30 to 35 degrees Celsius (86 to 95 degrees Fahrenheit).

The blue waters of the Tyrrhenian Sea tempt you to cool down, and the city's beaches, including the famed Scilla and Costa Viola, transform into bustling concentrations of activity.

During this time, Reggio Calabria holds a slew of vibrant festivals and activities, including the Riace Bronzes Festival, which honors the famed ancient Greek statues unearthed off the city's shore. The event includes art displays, live performances, and traditional music and dance.

You may also participate in water activities such as snorkeling, diving, and windsurfing, or take a boat excursion to the Aeolian Islands, a breathtaking archipelago famed for its volcanic scenery and beautiful seas.

For a taste of local culture, head to Scilla, a picturesque fishing hamlet where you can meander through its small alleys, eat fresh seafood, and observe the famed Chianalea neighborhood, with its colorful buildings pouring down to the sea.

Pack sunscreen, swimsuits, and lightweight clothing to keep cool and comfortable during the summer. Enjoy the vibrant environment, bathe in the Mediterranean sun, and make wonderful moments along the shore of Reggio Calabria.

Autumn Charms

As the summer heat passes away, fall is a wonderful time to visit Reggio Calabria. Between September and November, the city gets pleasant temperatures ranging from 20 to 25 degrees Celsius (68 to 77 degrees Fahrenheit). The summer throngs decrease, making for a more peaceful and personal atmosphere.

During this season, you may visit the adjacent Aspromonte National Park to see the spectacular fall foliage that covers the mountains in vivid hues. Take magnificent excursions along the park's paths, visit charming hillside villages like as Gerace and Stilo, and enjoy the fresh air.

Autumn also offers cultural events and festivals, such as the Grape Harvest Festival, which allows you to immerse yourself in local traditions while tasting the region's famous wines.

Participate in grape stomping, see traditional dances, and eat seasonal delicacies like chestnuts and mushrooms, which are abundant during this time.

For history buffs, fall is the best season to see the ancient remains of Locri Epizephiri, an important archeological site from the Magna Graecia period. The colder weather makes it easier to explore the remains and learn about the city's intriguing history.

With fewer people and excellent weather, fall provides a tranquil retreat with several possibilities to interact with nature, enjoy local traditions, and see Reggio Calabria's historical beauties.

Winter Wonders.

Although winter is the off-peak season in Reggio Calabria, it nonetheless has its own distinct appeal. From December to February, temperatures range between 10 and 15 degrees Celsius (50 and 59 degrees Fahrenheit).

Although chilly, the city is still quite temperate when compared to other regions of Europe, making it a desirable winter destination.

Winter visitors to Reggio Calabria may take their time exploring the city's historical and cultural attractions. The Cathedral of Reggio Calabria, which is dedicated to Saint Paul, is a must-see during this period. Admire its gorgeous architecture and rich artworks while taking in the calm of the season.

Stroll around the city center's calm streets, which are lit up with festive lights and decorations, and browse the local stores for one-of-a-kind presents and souvenirs. The winter months are ideal for enjoying the city's gastronomic wonders, which range from robust meals like 'nduja pasta to comforting soups and stews.

Warm up at the city's historic cafés with a cup of creamy Italian hot chocolate or a freshly prepared espresso. Take the opportunity to explore the Museo Nazionale della Magna Grecia, an archeological museum that displays ancient Greek artifacts and offers an intriguing peek into the region's past.

Winter is also an ideal time to explore the surrounding countryside. Take a lovely trip through the Calabrian region, which has rolling hills and stunning scenery.

The Aspromonte Mountains, covered in snow, provide options for winter trekking and skiing.

Reggio Calabria's winter ambiance, with its serene mood and cultural attractions, offers a one-of-a-kind and intimate experience for those seeking a gentler vacation.

Reggio Calabria, Italy, invites visitors year-round with its distinct combination of history, natural beauty, and cultural diversity. If you like the colorful ambiance of summer, the moderate temperatures of spring and autumn, or the calm charm of winter, there is an ideal season to come. Consider your particular interests and the experiences you want, and arrange your vacation accordingly.

Reggio Calabria enthusiastically awaits your arrival, promising to amaze you with its warm hospitality, stunning scenery, and authentic Italian experiences.

Why Choose Reggio Calabria as Your Next Travel Destination

Looking for an intriguing vacation spot that blends breathtaking natural scenery, a rich history, and genuine Italian culture?

Look no farther than Reggio Calabria, Italy. Nestled on the toe of the Italian boot, this dynamic city provides a mesmerizing blend of historic ruins, magnificent coastline, delectable cuisine, and welcoming friendliness.

Here are reasons why you should make Reggio Calabria your next trip destination.

1. **Unspoilt Beauty:**

Reggio Calabria has some of the most pristine and breathtaking natural beauty in Italy. The region is endowed with breathtaking mountain ranges, lush forests, and unspoiled coasts.

Aspromonte National Park, located just a short drive from the city, is a nature lover's heaven, with gorgeous hiking routes, gushing waterfalls, and breathtaking panoramic views.

2. Magnificent Scenic Drives:

Take picturesque drives along the beautiful coastal roads, including as the famed Costa Viola, which runs from Scilla to Bagnara Calabra.

This scenic road provides stunning views of the Tyrrhenian Sea, with its crystal-clear waters reflecting off the craggy rocks. Along the journey, you'll see picturesque fishing villages, vineyards, and olive orchards, offering plenty of possibilities for great photo stops.

3. Historical Wonders:

Reggio Calabria has a rich past, and history fans will be fascinated by the city's archeological riches. The Riace Bronzes, famous ancient Greek statues unearthed in the seas surrounding Riace and regarded marvels of art, are on exhibit at the National Archaeological Museum.

Explore the remnants of ancient Greek colonies like Locri Epizephiri and Caulonia to learn about Magna Graecia's rich cultural legacy.

4. Fascinating Museums:

Explore Reggio Calabria's diverse cultural legacy through its great museums.

The National Archaeological Museum holds an extensive collection of Magna Graecian items, including ancient Greek and Roman sculptures, ceramics, and jewelry.

The Regional Museum of Calabria provides insights into the region's history, art, and customs via displays ranging from ancient antiquities to modern works of art.

5. **Delicious Cuisine:**

Enjoy the delectable tastes of Calabrian food. Reggio Calabria is known for its genuine and hearty cuisine made with fresh, locally sourced ingredients. Try the famed 'nduja, a spicy spreadable salami produced with locally cultivated Calabrian chili peppers.

Enjoy seafood delicacies such as swordfish, anchovies, and sardines, which are plentiful along the shore. Don't miss out on trying the unusual Calabrian red chili pepper, known as the Calabrese diavolicchio, which lends a spicy bite to numerous recipes.

6. **Warm Hospitality:**

Enjoy the real warmth and kindness of the Calabrians. The inhabitants are noted for being kind and accommodating, making you feel right at home from the time you arrive.

Even if you're visiting the city's lively markets, dining at a family-run trattoria, or simply strolling down the promenade, you'll be greeted with a grin and open arms.

7. Beautiful Beaches:

Reggio Calabria has a long coastline with beautiful beaches and secret coves. Relax on the golden beaches of Scilla, a beautiful fishing community famous for its gorgeous beach and the legend of the sea monster Scylla.

Visit Bova Marina, a lovely beach with rich flora and crystal-clear seas ideal for swimming and sunbathing. Tropea, a short drive from Reggio Calabria, is another beach paradise, with stunning cliffs, blue waves, and a lively town center.

8. Charming Villages:

Explore the lovely villages that dot the Calabrian countryside, each with its own distinct personality and charm. Visit Gerace, a historic hilltop town nestled on the slopes of the Aspromonte Mountains. Lose yourself in its small alleyways lined with centuries-old houses and take in the spectacular views of the surrounding countryside.

Stroll through Badolato's charming streets, a well-preserved historic town with traditional architecture and a lovely ambiance that transports you back to the region's past.

9. Festivals and Traditions:

Participate in the active local culture by attending Reggio Calabria's vivid festivals and celebrations. During Holy Week, the city comes alive with parades, music, and fireworks.

Witness the colorful processions and religious rites. Join the Tarantella Power music and dance event, which celebrates the region's rich folk culture. Witness traditional skills like ceramics and cloth weaving, and learn about historic practices passed down through centuries.

10. Outdoor Adventures:

Reggio Calabria offers a variety of activities to satisfy adventurers' appetites for adrenaline. Explore Aspromonte National Park's raw beauty via its large network of hiking paths suitable for all skill levels. Admire the park's varied flora and fauna, which includes rare orchids and elusive animals like the Apennine wolf and golden eagle.

Go horseback riding in the countryside, passing through scenic landscapes and admiring panoramic vistas. For water enthusiasts, take exhilarating boat cruises around the coast to find secret caverns, snorkel in pristine seas, and even try your hand at fishing.

11. **Authentic Local Products:**

Reggio Calabria is full with one-of-a-kind local items that make excellent mementos. Explore the world of Calabrian artistry and take home classic ceramics that have been delicately hand-painted with exquisite motifs. Admire the skilled workmanship of local textile weavers, who produce magnificent textiles on traditional looms. T

aste the region's well-known olive oil, prepared from locally grown olives, and enjoy the powerful flavors of Calabrian wines, created from grapes cultivated in the Mediterranean climate and fertile land.

12. **Easy Access to Other Destinations:**

Reggio Calabria's strategic position gives it an excellent starting point for visiting other intriguing places in southern Italy.

Take a short ferry trip across the Strait of Messina to Sicily, where you may visit the historic city of Messina or continue on to the picturesque villages of Taormina and Syracuse.

Visit the Aeolian Islands, a volcanic archipelago renowned for its magnificent scenery and colorful culture. Alternatively, visit the scenic villages of the Calabrian area, such as Tropea with its breathtaking cliffside views or Pizzo, known for its exquisite tartufo ice cream and old castle.

Reggio Calabria is an ideal combination of natural beauty, historical treasures, delectable food, and kind friendliness. This charming city has something for everyone, whether you want to relax on gorgeous beaches, immerse yourself in culture, or embark on exhilarating outdoor experiences.

Choose Reggio Calabria as your next holiday destination and embark on an extraordinary adventure through one of Italy's hidden jewels. Immerse yourself in its pristine beauty, rich history, delectable cuisine, and friendly residents.

Reggio Calabria is eager to capture and inspire you with its various and amazing experiences.

The Landmarks and Must-See Top attractions in Reggio Calabria

When you visit Reggio Calabria, Italy, you will discover a city rich in history, culture, and natural beauty.

Here are the must-see monuments and top attractions in Reggio Calabria that tourists will enjoy exploring, each with engaging nuances that will make their stay genuinely unforgettable.

1. Piazza Italia

Begin your adventure in the center of the city by visiting Piazza Italia. This colorful area, surrounded by gorgeous buildings and bustling eateries, is the ideal place to start the day.

Take a seat at one of the outside tables, get a typical Italian espresso, and enjoy the lively environment of folks going about their day.

2. **Riace Bronzes.**

The Riace Bronzes are just a short walk from Piazza Italia and will leave you in amazement. These famous ancient Greek sculptures, discovered by chance in the seas of Riace in 1972, are regarded as one of the most significant archaeological findings of the twentieth century.

Admire the lifelike representations of the two warrior figurines, which have been painstakingly sculpted with stunning detail.

3. **Aragonese Castle.**

As you go through the streets of Reggio Calabria, be sure to visit the majestic Aragonese castle. Built in the 15th century, this historic stronghold boldly sits on a hill overlooking the city and provides panoramic views of the glittering Strait of Messina.

Wander inside its old walls, climb the towers, and imagine the previous stories that reverberate throughout its stone halls.

4. **National Archaeological Museum of Reggio Calabria**.

Visit the National Archaeological Museum of Reggio Calabria to indulge your interest in history and archaeology. You'll find an extraordinary collection of items from ancient Magna Graecia, a territory previously populated by Greek people.

Admire the magnificent Greek vases with mythological images, the delicate gold jewelry, and the elaborate mosaics depicting ancient legends.

5. **Falcomatà Longomare.**

To explore the region's natural beauty, take a leisurely stroll along the Lungomare Falcomatà. This lovely promenade runs along the city's shoreline, providing spectacular views of the crystal-clear waters of the Ionian Sea and the majestic silhouette of Mount Etna on the Sicilian horizon. Enjoy the invigorating sea breeze, listen to the waves smashing on the coast, and let nature's beauty surround you.

6. Aspromonte National Park.

For an escape into the nature, head beyond the municipal boundaries to Aspromonte National Park. This beautiful nature reserve is ideal for outdoor lovers.

Lace up your hiking boots and explore the network of paths that meander through deep woods, lead to scenic waterfalls, and provide panoramic views of the craggy highlands. Keep a watch out for the park's diverse fauna, which includes wild boar, deer, and golden eagles.

7. Locri Epizephyrii.

Experience the ancient past at the archeological site of Locri Epizephyrii. Walk through the remains of this once-vibrant Greek city, allowing your imagination to transport you back to a period when it was a thriving hub of trade and culture. Admire the ruins of temples, residences, and the well-preserved amphitheater, which once reverberated with spectators' cries.

8. Bergamot Museum.

The Bergamot Museum in the lovely town of Reggio di Calabria offers a one-of-a-kind cultural experience. Discover the intriguing history of the bergamot fruit, a citrus type that thrives in the area and is required for the manufacturing of the well-known Italian perfume.

Learn about its cultivation, extraction methods, and importance to the local economy.

9. Cathedral of Reggio Calabria.

History fans will enjoy a visit to the Cathedral of Reggio Calabria, a spectacular architectural jewel that reflects the city's rich history. Step inside this majestic Norman-style church and be impressed by its soaring columns, rich paintings, and breathtaking mosaics depicting holy subjects. Take a minute to meditate in the tranquil setting and enjoy the artistry that went into constructing this hallowed spot.

10. The Fata Morgana Ethnographic Museum.

Take a leisurely stroll around the Fata Morgana Ethnographic Museum, housed in a beautiful palace in the center of the city. This intriguing museum provides insight into the Calabrians' daily lives, traditions, and cultural heritage.

Explore the exhibitions displaying traditional crafts, clothing, and household objects to obtain a better knowledge of the region's diverse cultural tapestry.

11. Casa Natale di Umberto Boccioni.

If you enjoy modern art, don't miss the opportunity to see the Casa Natale di Umberto Boccioni. This modest museum is devoted to the renowned Italian painter and sculptor and exhibits a selection of his works, which provide insight into the early twentieth-century Futurist Movement. Admire Boccioni's dynamic sculptures and bright paintings, which encapsulate modernism and the spirit of the moment.

12. The Francesco Cilea Community Theatre.

Finish your tour of Reggio Calabria with the Teatro Comunale Francesco Cilea. This old opera building, named for the renowned composer Francesco Cilea, is a genuine jewel of the city.

Attend a concert at this magnificent venue and immerse yourself in the magical world of music and drama.

The Teatro Comunale presents a diversified program that includes operas, ballets, and concerts, showcasing exceptional artists and providing a memorable cultural experience.

Allow yourself to be enchanted by Reggio Calabria's rich history, natural marvels, and dynamic cultural environment as you visit these sites and must-see attractions.

From ancient treasures such as the Riace Bronzes and Locri Epizephyrii to spectacular vistas along the Lungomare Falcomatà and immersive experiences at the National Archaeological Museum, each step you take will expand your admiration for this wonderful place.

Even if you're a history buff, an art lover, or simply want to reconnect with nature, Reggio Calabria has a tapestry of experiences that will make an everlasting impression on your journey.

The Weather and Climate of Reggio Calabria

Reggio Calabria has a Mediterranean climate that provides a great combination of warm summers, moderate winters, and good weather all year.

As you visit this lovely city, allow me to offer a realistic image of the weather and environment that await you.

Your journey to Reggio Calabria begins with unquestionably beautiful summers. The sun smiles at you and warms the city with its beautiful rays. Imagine yourself wandering down the magnificent Lungomare Falcomatà, the city's lung, while a pleasant sea wind transports the aroma of salt and the music of breaking waves.

During the summer, temperatures hover in the mid-80s Fahrenheit (upper 20s Celsius), making the Ionian Sea's sandy coasts ideal for sunbathing. Don't forget to wear sunscreen while you bask in the sun and enjoy the Mediterranean serenity.

As the beautiful colors of summer fade into autumn, Reggio Calabria enters a season of pleasant temperatures and quiet. The fall air is crisp, making it an ideal time to explore the city's historical landmarks and sample the local food.

Imagine walking through the historic center's small streets, feeling the sun's soft warmth on your face while sipping a steaming cup of freshly prepared espresso. The typical temperature in the fall varies from the mid-60s to low 70s Fahrenheit (high teens to low 20s Celsius), making it a great climate for your travels.

Winter arrives in Reggio Calabria with a soft hug, providing a welcome break from the colder temperatures found elsewhere in Europe. The city has moderate winters, with typical temperatures ranging from the mid-50s to low-60s Fahrenheit (high teens Celsius). Imagine yourself wandering along the Piazza Italia, decked with dazzling lights and festive decorations, immersed in the joy of the holiday season.

Indulge in traditional dishes like as nduja and cipolle di Tropea, which will warm your spirit with their rich tastes. While snow is uncommon here, the nearby Aspromonte Mountains may be coated with a magnificent white blanket, providing a picturesque background for your winter pursuits.

Spring blooms in Reggio Calabria, transforming the city into a vivid spectrum of hues. Consider strolling around the Giardino Botanico dell'Università, the city's botanical garden, while aromatic blooms scent the air.

Temperatures gradually climb, with averages ranging from the high 50s to low 70s Fahrenheit (mid-teens to low 20s Celsius), making it a perfect time to explore the city's natural beauties.

Take a leisurely walk through Aspromonte National Park, see the gushing waterfalls, and let the revitalizing energy of spring awaken your senses.

Reggio Calabria enjoys a mild climate all year, thanks to its closeness to the sea and the soft impact of the Mediterranean. The city receives a reasonable quantity of rainfall, primarily throughout the autumn and winter months, which refreshes the landscapes and sustains lush flora.

Reggio Calabria is a city where the weather welcomes you like an old friend, asking you to enjoy each season's particular attractions.

From the warmth of the sun-drenched summers to the mildness of the winters, this Mediterranean gem's environment perfectly compliments its rich history, cultural legacy, and beautiful landscape.

So pack your bags, travel to Reggio Calabria, and immerse yourself in a world where the weather and temperature are as welcoming as the residents.

Chapter 4: Travel Tips and Resources to Reggio Calabria

The Visa Requirements and Entry Regulations to Reggio Calabria

Welcome to Reggio Calabria, a charming city in southern Italy.

Even if you're planning a vacation or a longer stay, it's essential to educate yourself with visa requirements and entry regulations to guarantee a smooth and hassle-free journey.

This detailed guide will provide you with all of the information you need to complete the procedure smoothly.

1. **Visa Requirements:**

To enter Reggio Calabria, Italy, you must evaluate if you require a visa based on your nationality. Italy is a signatory to the Schengen Agreement, which enables visa-free travel for citizens of specified countries. However, people of other nations must get a visa before to their visit.

To determine if you require a visa, contact the Italian embassy or consulate in your own country or visit their official website.

2. Schengen Area:

Reggio Calabria is a member of the Schengen Area, which includes 26 European nations with open borders. If you are a citizen of a Schengen member state, you can enter Italy without a visa and remain for up to 90 days within a 180-day period.

Make sure your passport is valid for at least six months after your scheduled travel date.

3. Visa Application Process:

If you need a visa to enter Italy, you must apply through the Italian embassy or consulate in your home country.

The procedure often include filling out an application form and submitting required papers such as a valid passport, proof of lodging, trip itinerary, travel insurance, evidence of financial means, and a current passport-sized image. Check the embassy's website for a complete list of criteria.

4. **Schengen Visa Types:**

There are several types of Schengen visas, including tourist, business, student, and medical visas. Determine the objective of your visit and then apply for the appropriate visa type.

Tourist visas are the most porpular, and they allow you to visit Reggio Calabria and other regions of Italy for leisure.

5. **Visa Processing Times:**

Visa processing times vary based on the embassy or consulate in your home country and the time of year. It is best to apply well in advance of your intended trip to give enough time for processing.

In certain circumstances, processing time might be several weeks, so plan accordingly. Check with the embassy or consulate for an estimated processing time.

6. **Entry Regulations:**

When traveling to Reggio Calabria, Italy, make sure you have the following documents ready for immigration:

- ❖ **Valid Passport:**

Your passport should be valid for at least six months after your planned visit. Make sure there are at least two blank pages for entry and exit stamps.

- ❖ **Visa:**

If you need a visa, be sure it is legitimate and fits the purpose of your visit. Check the validity dates and any limitations connected with your visa.

- ❖ **Return Ticket:**

Immigration officials may request documentation of a return or onward ticket to demonstrate that you intend to depart Italy within the time period specified. Make sure you have a verified itinerary or booking information.

- ❖ **Accommodation Details:**

Bring details concerning your stay in Reggio Calabria, such as hotel bookings or a letter of invitation if staying with friends or relatives.

The address and contact information should be easily accessible.

- ❖ **Sufficient Funds:**

Bring enough cash or a valid credit card to cover your spending during your stay. The amount necessary may vary, but a basic rule is to have at least €50-€100 every day.

7. **Customs and Immigration:**

When you arrive in Reggio Calabria, you will travel through customs and immigration.

Prepare for the following procedures:

- ❖ **Passport Control:**

Bring your passport and visa (if applicable) to the immigration officer for scrutiny and entrance stamping. Answer any inquiries about the purpose and duration of your stay with honesty and confidence.

- ❖ **Customs Declaration:**

Fill out a customs declaration form as needed. Declare any things that exceed the duty-free allowance, as well as any restricted or forbidden goods. Familiarize oneself with customs regulations to avoid problems.

- ❖ **Baggage Inspection:**

Customs inspectors may randomly check your luggage. Make sure you're not carrying any forbidden things like narcotics, weapons, or counterfeit products. It is best to pack your items in an orderly manner for simple examination.

- ❖ **Health standards:**

Italy may have unique health standards, particularly during times of health emergency. Check whether any immunization certificates or health declarations are required for entrance.

8. **Extend Your Stay:**

If you want to stay over the 90-day limit within the Schengen Area, you must inform the local immigration officials in Reggio Calabria or the nearby Questura (police station) before your visa expires. Request an extension and offer legitimate grounds for your extended stay. Extensions are only given in rare situations.

Visiting Reggio Calabria, Italy, is an exciting experience, but you must understand the visa requirements and entrance laws to guarantee a smooth admission and stay.

Determine if you require a visa based on your nationality, and apply for the right type. Familiarize yourself with the Schengen Area laws and make sure you have the essential documentation and finances for your travel.

Follow the customs and immigration procedures when you arrive, and if you need to extend your stay, notify the local immigration officials right once.

By following this comprehensive guide, you'll be well-prepared to discover the beauty of Reggio Calabria and make unforgettable experiences in this delightful Italian city.

Packing Essentials: What You Should Bring on Your Trip to Reggio Calabria

Traveling to Reggio Calabria, Italy, offers an adventure full of breathtaking scenery, rich history, and delectable cuisine. As you plan your vacation, it's critical to pack strategically so that you have everything you need to make the most of your stay in this lovely part of the globe.

From basic necessities to trendy accessories, here's a list of things you should pack to Reggio Calabria.

1. **Comfortable Clothes:**

Reggio Calabria's Mediterranean environment provides warm, sunny summers and moderate winters, so bring a wardrobe that can adapt to changing weather conditions.

In the summer, use lightweight, breathable materials such as cotton and linen. Pack shorts, t-shirts, sundresses, and light pants.

Don't forget to pack appropriate walking shoes for exploring the city's cobblestone streets, as well as beach sandals. During the cooler months, carry a light jacket or sweater to layer.

2. Swimsuit and Beach Essentials:

Reggio Calabria has gorgeous beaches along its coastline, so bring your swimsuits and beach needs. Don't miss your chance to swim in the Mediterranean Sea's crystal-clear waters.

Pack your favorite swimsuit or trunks, a beach towel, high-SPF sunscreen, a sun hat, and sunglasses. Consider taking a lightweight beach cover-up for additional sun protection.

3. Travel Documents:

Prepare your travel paperwork before departing for Reggio Calabria. Make sure you have your passport, visa (if applicable), and any essential identity cards. Make many copies of these documents and store them in a secure location.

It's also a good idea to save digital copies to your phone or cloud storage. In addition, obtain travel insurance that covers medical emergencies and loss of valuables.

4. Language Guide, Maps:

While many Reggio Calabrians understand English, possessing a basic Italian language guide might improve your vacation experience.

It demonstrates your eagerness to engage with the people and opens the door to genuine encounters. Carry a pocket-sized phrasebook or download a language app to your smartphone.

Maps or a reputable navigation program are also required for touring the city and making your way around its attractive streets and attractions.

5. **Electrical Adapters and Chargers:**

Italy utilizes Europlug Type C and Type L electrical outlets, so bring the proper adapters for your electronic equipment.

It's also a good idea to have a portable charger so you can keep your gadgets charged while visiting the city. Consider purchasing a universal adaptor that can fit multiple plug types for future journeys.

6. **Medications and First-aid Kits:**

If you use prescription drugs, be sure you have enough to last the whole trip. It's also a good idea to have a basic first aid kit containing bandages, pain killers, antihistamines, and other personal prescriptions you might require.

In the event of an emergency, become familiar with the locations of local pharmacies and hospitals. Remember to save your drugs in their original packaging, as well as any essential prescriptions or medical documentation.

7. **Money and Banking:**

Before you go, notify your bank of your trip intentions to avoid any card complications. To be more convenient, carry a combination of cash and credit/debit cards.

While most businesses in Reggio Calabria take credit cards, it's a good idea to keep cash on hand for smaller stores, local markets, and transportation. ATMs are widely distributed across the city, however be mindful of any associated costs.

Consider carrying a money belt or a lockable travel wallet to protect your belongings.

8. Travel Adapters and Converters:

Italy uses 230V electricity, therefore if your electronic gadgets demand a different voltage, pack a travel adapter and converter.

This ensures that your gadgets may be charged securely and without damage. Check your devices' voltage requirements and select a converter that meets your needs.

9. Daypacks or Tote Bags:

A tiny daypack or tote bag is quite useful for day excursions and sightseeing. It lets you to carry necessary objects while leaving your hands free. Invest in a lightweight, comfortable, and safe bag that complements your own style.

Pack a reusable water bottle, food, a camera, a guidebook or map, and a light jacket or scarf in case of unexpected weather changes.

10. Personal Care Items:

Don't forget to pack your personal care goods, such as toiletries, skincare products, and any prescriptions or hygiene supplies you need.

Remember to follow airline limits for liquid volume and store them in a transparent, resealable bag. Consider packing bug repellent, hand sanitizer, wet wipes, and a compact travel mirror for extra convenience.

Packing for your journey to Reggio Calabria is an exciting aspect of planning your experience. Consider these important goods, such as comfortable clothes, swimsuits, travel papers, language guides, adapters, prescriptions, money, personal care products, and more, to ensure that you have all you need to enjoy your time in this interesting place.

Remember to travel light, appreciate the local culture, and enjoy every second of your trip to Reggio Calabria.

Even if you're seeing the city's historical monuments, relaxing on its stunning beaches, or enjoying in wonderful local food, having the appropriate basics will make your vacation memorable and delightful.

Have a good trip!

Health and Safety Tips for Travelers Visiting Reggio Calabria

Welcome to Reggio Calabria, Italy! As you go to this lovely place, it is critical that you prioritize your health and safety.

To guarantee a comfortable and worry-free vacation, we have created a list of vital health and safety tips designed exclusively for travelers like you.

1. **Prepare for your Journey:**

Before embarking on your vacation, ensure that you have comprehensive travel insurance that covers medical expenditures and emergencies. Familiarize yourself with the local healthcare system and have crucial contact information ready.

It is also a good idea to include a small first aid kit with bandages, pain killers, and any prescription prescriptions you may need.

2. **Stay Hydrated:**

The warm Mediterranean environment and outdoor activities in Reggio Calabria may put you at risk of dehydration. Carry a refillable water bottle and drink lots of water all day.

Remember to drink bottled water rather than tap water. You may also eat local citrus fruits like oranges and lemons, which are both refreshing and hydrating.

3. Protect yourself from the Sun.

Reggio Calabria's sun may be harsh, especially during the summer months. It is critical to protect oneself from damaging UV radiation. Wear a wide-brimmed hat that covers your face, neck, and ears.

Invest in an excellent pair of sunglasses that offer 100% UV protection to safeguard your eyes. Apply a broad-spectrum sunscreen with a minimum SPF of 30 to all exposed skin, including your face, arms, and legs. Reapply sunscreen every two hours, particularly after swimming or sweating. To avoid sunburn and heatstroke, seek cover during peak sunshine hours, which are typically 11 a.m. to 3 p.m.

4. **Maintain Personal Hygiene.**

Maintaining personal cleanliness is essential for your health, especially while traveling. Wash your hands often with soap and water for at least 20 seconds, particularly before meals and after visiting public restrooms.

Carry hand sanitizers containing at least 60% alcohol for occasions when soap and water are not readily accessible. Apply hand sanitizer after contacting surfaces like doorknobs, handrails, or public transportation. Avoid touching your face to reduce the danger of spreading germs.

5. **Take Precautions against Mosquitos:**

Mosquitoes can be drawn to Reggio Calabria by its rich flora and proximity to bodies of water, especially during the warmer months.

Wear long-sleeved clothes and long pants to avoid mosquito bites, especially in the evening and early morning, when mosquitoes are most active. Apply insect repellents or other active chemicals to exposed skin and clothes.

Consider staying in places with window screens or sleeping under mosquito netting. If you are extremely susceptible to mosquito bites, speak with your doctor about suitable preventative measures.

6. **Practice Food and Water Safety.**

Italian cuisine is a lovely experience, but be sure the food and drink you eat are safe. Choose reputed restaurants and cafes that follow strict food handling and cleanliness guidelines.

Choose well-cooked and freshly prepared meals. Avoid raw or undercooked seafood and street food, since these may increase the risk of foodborne disease. Drink bottled or filtered water, and avoid ice cubes created with tap water.

Before eating, fruits and vegetables should be completely peeled or washed.

7. **Be Cautious with Street Vendors.**

While touring the bustling streets of Reggio Calabria, you may come across street sellers offering a variety of goods. To avoid pickpocketing or other forms of theft, use care and keep an eye on your surroundings. Keep your stuff safe and in sight at all times.

Consider utilizing a money belt or neck pouch to keep your valuables hidden.

It is advised that you keep your cash and critical documents in separate pockets or bags to reduce the effect of any potential loss.

8. Stay Informed About Local Laws and Customs:

To guarantee a trouble-free journey, become acquainted with the local laws and traditions of Reggio Calabria. It is crucial to respect Italy's distinct customs and traditions.

Dress modestly while visiting religious sites such as churches or basilicas, and adhere to any dress regulations that may be in place. Be cautious of your behavior in public areas, and refrain from engaging in actions that might be deemed rude or insulting.

It's always better to fit in and demonstrate cultural awareness.

9. Practice safe Transportation.

Whether you're taking public transit or renting a car, consider your safety. When using cabs, make sure the company is legal and reliable.

Ensure that the taxi has a functional meter or agree on a fare in advance. If you're driving, learn the local traffic rules and regulations. Always use seatbelts, and if you hire a car, make sure it is in good shape and adequately insured. Be aware of pedestrians and obey traffic signals and speed restrictions to ensure a safe ride.

Reggio Calabria is a remarkable combination of natural beauty, rich history, and welcoming friendliness.

Following these health and safety tips will help you have a memorable and worry-free trip.

Prioritize your well-being, learn about local laws and customs, and enjoy the beauty and culture of this fascinating country.

Chapter 5: Planning the Perfect Journey to Reggio Calabria

How to plan a Budget-friendly journey to Reggio Calabria

Going on a vacation to Reggio Calabria, Italy, may be an enjoyable experience without breaking the budget. This guide will assist you in planning a budget-friendly vacation to this attractive city, with an emphasis on essential areas such as accommodation, food, transportation, fun activities, budget management, and safety.

By following these tips, you will make the most of your journey while staying within your budget.

Accommodation:

Consider a few possibilities for economical lodgings in Reggio Calabria. To save money on commuting, look for affordable hotels, hostels, or bed & breakfasts in the city center or near public transit, such as the Central Station.

Hotel Continental, Hotel Lungomare, and B&B H24 are some of the suggested cheap lodgings in Reggio Calabria.

Consider reserving in early to get better bargains, and check costs on reputable travel companies like reserving.com or Airbnb. Another cost-effective option is to look into vacation rentals or homestays, which not only give affordable housing but also allow you to immerse yourself in the local culture.

Food:

Immerse yourself in the tastes of Italy while staying within your budget. Reggio Calabria has a range of affordable eating alternatives. Seek for local trattorias, family-run eateries, or street food carts that serve real Italian cuisine at moderate pricing. For low-cost dining options, walk around Via Marina or Via Aschenez.

Opt for fixed-price lunch menus, often known as "menu del giorno," which frequently comprise a range of meals at a reduced cost. These meals often include pasta, meat or fish, side dishes, and a beverage. Osteria dei Sani, Trattoria La

Risacca, and Pizzeria Amicizia are some of Reggio Calabria's popular budget-friendly eateries.

Take advantage of local markets and grocery stores, such as Mercato di Catona, to buy fresh vegetables, bread, and cheese for picnics or self-prepared dinners, which may be a fun and inexpensive way to sample local cuisine.

Transportation:

To get around Reggio Calabria on a budget, use the city's excellent public transit system. Buses are a quick and inexpensive way to move about the city and local attractions.

The AMT Reggio Calabria maintains a large bus network that connects the city center to many districts and attractions. Consider obtaining a rechargeable transit card, such as the Metromare Card, to get lower rates. This card may be used on both buses and trains.

Walking is also an excellent option to explore the city center and neighboring monuments, saving money and allowing you to absorb up the local culture. If you want to visit sights outside of the city, study and compare pricing for public transportation choices such as trains or shared taxis to determine the most cost-effective route to your destination.

For example, the rail is a handy and economical way to get to nearby cities such as Scilla or Villa San Giovanni.

Fun Activities:

Reggio Calabria has a variety of low-cost activities that allow you to explore the city's rich history and natural beauty. Begin by visiting the National Archaeological Museum of Reggio Calabria, which houses the famed Riace Bronzes and depicts the region's historical history.

Students, seniors, and families can get a subsidized entrance to the museum. Take a leisurely stroll down the coastal promenade, Lungomare Falcomatà, and see the beautiful views of the Strait of Messina and the Sicilian coastline.

Walk through the historical center's small lanes and uncover hidden jewels including churches, piazzas, and local markets. The Cathedral of Reggio Calabria and the Church of Saint Gaetano Catanoso are worth visiting. Consider visiting the gorgeous beaches nearby, such as

Scilla or Pellaro, which are easily accessible and provide a refreshing break.

These beaches are free to use, and you can pack your own towels and refreshments for a low-cost beach day.

Budget Management:

To properly manage your budget, you must plan your spending in advance. Create a daily budget that includes monies for lodging, meals, transportation, activities, and unexpected costs.

Set reasonable expectations by researching the average costs of various commodities and services in Reggio Calabria. Take advantage of free or low-cost sights and activities, such as visiting parks like Villa Genoese Zerbi or attending local festivals that frequently highlight the region's cultural legacy. Walking tours, such as the Free Walking Tour Reggio Calabria, are an inexpensive way to discover the city while learning about its history and culture. Look for discounts or special deals on attractions, museums, and transportation passes.

To stay within your budget, keep track of your spending with a budgeting tool or a basic notepad.

Safety:

While Reggio Calabria is typically a secure city, you should always prioritize your own safety when traveling.

Take simple measures, such as avoiding poorly lit locations at night, remaining alert of your surroundings, and protecting your possessions. Be wary of pickpockets, particularly in busy locations and on public transit.

It is advised that you store your possessions in a money belt or a safe bag. Stay up to date on local news and follow any travel advisories or advice issued by your embassy or consulate. To provide peace of mind during your travels, it is recommended that you get travel insurance that covers medical emergencies and trip cancellations.

In the event of an emergency, educate yourself with the local emergency numbers and the location of the nearest hospitals or medical institutions.

Planning a budget-friendly journey to Reggio Calabria, Italy allows you to experience the city's beauty, history, and culture without breaking the bank.

You can have a memorable and budget-friendly experience in this captivating Italian destination by carefully selecting affordable accommodations, enjoying local cuisine sensibly, taking advantage of public transportation, participating in budget-friendly activities, effectively managing your funds, and prioritizing your safety.

Reggio Calabria greets you with its picturesque alleys, archaeological riches, breathtaking coastline, and delectable cuisine—all while remaining within your budget.

Happy travels!

How to Plan a Family-Friendly Vacation to Reggio Calabria.

Welcome to the wonderful city of Reggio Calabria in Italy! Reggio Calabria, known for its beautiful coastline, rich history, and wonderful food, has a wealth of family-friendly activities.

To achieve a well-rounded trip, meticulous planning is required. This guide will walk you through all areas of your trip, including lodging, food, transportation, family-friendly activities, budget, and safety.

By taking these things into account, you may provide a smooth and delightful experience for the entire family, resulting in lifelong memories.

Accommodation.

Reggio Calabria has a variety of family-friendly lodging options to meet diverse needs. Consider vacationing in a hotel or resort designed exclusively for families.

Look for large rooms or suites with enough space for everyone to unwind. Many family-friendly hotels have amenities such as swimming pools, kids' clubs, and playgrounds, ensuring that your children are amused during your visit.

Alternatively, renting an apartment or villa might give a more peaceful ambiance, as well as the convenience of having a kitchen to prepare meals. Consider staying in a central location, such as the waterfront or in the city center, for easy access to attractions and public transit.

Food.

Reggio Calabria is a culinary heaven, and sampling the local food is a vital part of any family-friendly vacation. Look for family-friendly eateries with different menus.

These places frequently serve a variety of foods to suit varied tastes, including alternatives for youngsters. Enjoy classic Calabrian delights like 'nduja, a spicy spreadable sausage, or fresh seafood dishes prepared with locally sourced ingredients.

Many restaurants offer high chairs, which make dining with small children more pleasant. Consider taking a cooking class or food tour developed exclusively for families, where you can learn about local products and traditional recipes while participating in hands-on culinary activities.

Transportation.

Reggio Calabria and its surroundings are quite easy to navigate, thanks to a variety of transit alternatives. Public transportation, such as buses and trams, is an inexpensive and quick method to travel around town.

Look for family-friendly transportation passes or tickets that provide discounts for kids. Renting a car allows you to explore the region at your own speed. Ensure that you have appropriate car seats for your children and follow local safety standards. Reggio Calabria is a pedestrian-friendly city, with several attractions within walking distance.

Consider exploring the city on foot or by renting bicycles, which allows you to find hidden jewels while spending quality time with your family.

Family-friendly Activities.

Reggio Calabria provides a variety of family-friendly activities for people of all ages and interests. Begin your tour in the National Archaeological Museum, where you and your family may see the world-renowned Riace Bronzes, ancient relics, and interactive displays that bring history to life.

The Museo dei Ragazzi (Children's Museum) is another must-see location, providing hands-on learning experiences and engaging activities to pique your children's interest.

For outdoor aficionados, a visit to Aspromonte National Park is essential. Take picturesque treks across stunning landscapes, enjoy picnics in nature, and learn about the region's unique biodiversity.

The park's visitor centers frequently provide guided tours and educational programs for families.

The Lungomare Falcomatà, a scenic promenade along the seaside, is ideal for leisurely walks or bike excursions. Enjoy breathtaking views of the sea, visit gelato shops, and let your children play in the approved playground spaces along the way.

Don't forget to take family photographs at the landmark "Piedigrotta Church," which is built into a rocky cliff.

Reggio Calabria has lovely beaches perfect for family relaxation and pleasure. Choose from Lido Comunale, Spiaggia degli Angeli, and Spiaggia di Pellaro, all of which have clean beaches, shallow seas, and a variety of water sports activities suited for children. Bring beach toys, umbrellas, and sunscreen to guarantee a relaxing day by the water.

Budget.

Traveling on a budget in Reggio Calabria is possible with proper planning. Look for inexpensive lodging choices such as guesthouses, bed & breakfasts, or budget hotels that provide comfort and convenience. Use local markets or grocery stores to stock up on fresh fruits, snacks, and picnic necessities, which may help you save money on meals.

Many sites, including parks and museums, provide cheap or free entrance to children. Exploring the city's natural beauties, such as parks and beaches, is generally free. Consider going during the shoulder seasons (spring or fall), when costs are lower and the weather remains good. Investigate local events or festivals, since they frequently provide cultural activities and entertainment alternatives that are free or have low admission costs.

Safety.

Reggio Calabria is a relatively secure city, however it's essential to emphasize safety throughout your family trip. Keep a watch on your stuff, particularly in congested regions or tourist destinations. When crossing roads, keep an eye out for cars and utilize marked pedestrian crossing points.

Check that your preferred lodging satisfies safety requirements and has enough security measures in place.

Familiarize yourself with emergency contact numbers and keep a list of area medical institutions. It is important to purchase travel insurance that covers medical emergencies and trip cancellations. Teach your children fundamental safety guidelines, such as remaining close to you in public areas and not approaching strangers. Encourage them to carry identification and emergency contact information.

By following these steps, you may have a worry-free and safe family vacation in Reggio Calabria.

When planning a family vacation to Reggio Calabria, you must consider lodging, food, transportation, family-friendly activities, budgets, and safety.

Reggio Calabria offers a variety of activities and experiences for people of all ages, ensuring that your family has a great journey. From touring intriguing museums to relaxing on lovely beaches and feasting in delectable food, the city has something for everyone.

You can make your family's vacation genuinely special by carefully planning your schedule, selecting family-friendly hotels, immersing yourself in local culture, managing your finances intelligently, and emphasizing safety.

Embrace the charm of Reggio Calabria and make memorable experiences together.

Enjoy your travels!

Chapter 6: Things to Do: Must-See Top Attractions in Reggio Calabria

Recommended Must-See Top Attraction in Reggio Calabria

Lungomare Falcomatà

Lungomare Falcomatà, located in the beautiful city of Reggio Calabria is a stunning waterfront promenade with a timeless appeal. This magnificent esplanade, which runs along the Strait of Messina, combines natural beauty with cultural legacy in a balanced way.

The Lungomare, lined by palm trees and filled with bright flower beds, offers spectacular views of the crystal-clear seas and the gorgeous Sicilian coastline in the distance.

Visitors to the promenade will come across fine cafés, exotic boutiques, and welcoming benches, all of which invite them to relax and reflect.

The Lungomare Falcomatà exemplifies Reggio Calabria's beauty, offering a beautiful environment for leisurely walks, romantic sunsets, and treasured memories.

Museo Archeologico Nazionale di Reggio Calabria

The Museo Archeologico Nazionale di Reggio Calabria is an interesting museum that has a diverse collection of ancient objects from the region.

The museum is well-known for its remarkable collection of ancient Greek treasures, including the famed Riace Bronzes, two hypnotic sculptures of Greek soldiers from the fifth century BC.

Visitors may marvel at a variety of archaeological findings, including as pottery, jewelry, and sculptures, which provide insights into Calabria's ancient history and culture.

The museum's displays are carefully arranged to provide a thorough overview of the region's history.

The Museo Archeologico Nazionale di Reggio Calabria, with its impressive exhibits and historical relevance, provides an immersive voyage into the ancient world.

Castello Aragonese

Castello Aragonese is a beautiful fortification rich in history and architectural magnificence. It sits on a rocky islet, overlooking the turquoise waves of the Tyrrhenian Sea and providing spectacular panoramic views of the surrounding countryside.

Originally erected by the Byzantines, the fortress was later enlarged by the Aragonese, who left an unmistakable stamp on its architecture.

Its enormous stone walls, fortified towers, and drawbridge provide a feeling of medieval grandeur. Inside, visitors may explore a maze of rooms, courtyards, and gardens, each showcasing a distinct aspect of the castle's fascinating history.

From its strategic position to its stunning architecture, Castello Aragonese is a testimony to the region's cultural legacy and provides a fascinating peek into Italy's medieval past.

Arena dello Stretto

Arena dello Stretto is a spectacular open-air amphitheater that captivates tourists with its breathtaking scenery and rich cultural legacy. Nestled on the banks of the Strait of Messina, the arena provides stunning views of the brilliant blue seas and the Sicilian coastline in the background.

With a seating capacity of thousands, the Arena dello Stretto is a notable venue for a wide range of events, including concerts, theatrical performances, and festivals.

Its sophisticated design mixes harmoniously with the natural beauty of the surroundings, providing a one-of-a-kind and fascinating environment.

If witnessing a musical spectacle or simply enjoying the architectural wonder, visitors to the Arena dello Stretto

have amazing experience

Museo Nazionale del Bergamotto

The Museo Nazionale del Bergamotto, located in Reggio Calabria, Italy, is a compelling institution dedicated to the region's famous bergamot fruit.

The museum, which spans three levels, provides visitors with an in-depth look into the cultural, historical, and economic significance of the bergamot.

The exhibitions highlight the fruit's growth, processing methods, and numerous uses in scent, cosmetics, and food.

Visitors may immerse themselves in the museum's aromatic ambiance, exploring the many fragrances and sensations connected with bergamot.

Engaging displays, interactive exhibits, and multimedia presentations make for an engaging learning experience.

The museum also offers seminars, lectures, and events to help visitors learn more about this amazing citrus fruit, making it a must-see site for those interested in Reggio Calabria's rich legacy.

Roghudi Vecchio

Roghudi Vecchio is a charming village set in the beautiful mountains of Reggio Calabria, Italy. This charming village is steeped in history and charm, providing a look into the region's rich cultural legacy.

The community is known for its stone buildings, small cobblestone lanes, and stunning views of the surrounding landscape.

Walking around Roghudi Vecchio is like stepping back in time, as the antique buildings and treasured customs create nostalgia. With its quiet environment and close-knit population, the hamlet emanates tranquillity.

Visitors may visit the local church, eat traditional Calabrian food, and take in the timeless beauty of Roghudi Vecchio's natural surroundings.

It's an exquisite place for people looking for a true Italian experience.

Spiaggia Gallico Marina

Spiaggia Gallico Marina in the coastal city of Reggio Calabria, Italy, is a captivating location with its natural beauty and tranquil atmosphere.

This beautiful beach has a unique combination of golden beaches, crystal-clear blue seas, and lush surrounding flora.

Spiaggia Gallico Marina's exquisite environment enables visitors to relax, soak in the Mediterranean sun, and enjoy the delights of the water.

The beach has great facilities, such as umbrellas, sun loungers, and seaside eateries, which ensure that beachgoers have a pleasant and pleasurable time. Even if you want peace and quiet, water activities, or just spectacular views, Spiaggia Gallico Marina is a charming coastal hideaway that promises wonderful experiences in the heart of southern Italy.

Spiaggia di Riace

Spiaggia di Riace is a breathtaking coastal gem that captivates tourists with its natural beauty and historical value.

Located along the Ionian Sea, this gorgeous beach features blue waters, golden beaches, and stunning views of the surrounding environment.

What distinguishes Spiaggia di Riace is its connection to the Riace Bronzes, ancient Greek sculptures unearthed nearby in 1972.

These exquisite statues, now housed in a museum, have become iconic representations of the area's rich cultural past.

Visitors to the beach may immerse themselves in history while enjoying the peaceful atmosphere and relaxing waves.

Spiaggia di Riace is a must-see site for beachgoers, history buffs, and those looking for a combination of natural beauty and archaeological treasures.

Spiaggia della Marinella

Spiaggia della Marinella is a beautiful coastal gem that captivates visitors with its natural beauty. With a little description, this lovely beach oozes peace and attractiveness.

The silky golden beaches are softly caressed by the turquoise waves of the Ionian Sea, providing a tranquil setting ideal for relaxation.

The beach is surrounded by rich Mediterranean flora and steep rocks, providing spectacular panoramic views.

Visitors may enjoy the warm Mediterranean sun, take soothing dives in the crystal-clear waters, or hike the neighboring picturesque paths.

Spiaggia della Marinella is an exquisite hideaway where nature's magnificence merges with the charm of the Italian coastline, making it a must-see destination for both beachgoers and wildlife aficionados.

Spiaggia Di Scilla

Spiaggia Di Scilla, located in the charming coastal town of Scilla in Reggio Calabria is a gorgeous beach that exemplifies Mediterranean beauty.

With crystal-clear blue waves softly lapping against golden dunes, it provides a tranquil and picturesque backdrop.

The beach, located beneath the magnificent Ruffo Castle and flanked by spectacular cliffs, is a postcard-perfect resort.

Visitors may relax in the warm Mediterranean sun while admiring the stunning views of the Tyrrhenian Sea. Spiaggia Di Scilla also has wonderful amenities, such as seaside taverns and restaurants that provide superb local food.

Even if you want to relax, sunbathe, or explore the beautiful town, Spiaggia Di Scilla offers an amazing beach experience in one of Italy's most beautiful coastal locations.

Chapter 7: Exploring Reggio Calabria

Historic Walking Areas in Reggio Calabria

Lungomare Falcomatà

Reggio Calabria's beachfront spans about two kilometers in a broad sky and sea scene.

On the background of the Strait of Messina, there is a monument to the Greek goddess Athena in honor of the then-king of Italy, Vittorio Emanuele III, as well as a monument commemorating Italy's victory in World War I.

A walk along the seashore in Reggio Calabria is not to be missed. Beautiful promenade, serene, well-kept flora. A breathtaking view with the Strait of Messina and Etna in the background.

Many pubs across the street sell coffee.

Cultural Tour in Reggio Calabria

Guided Tour of the Museum of Reggio Calabria and the City

Phone number: +1 855 275 5071

Myths and fiction, history, culture, and folklore all come together in a single place. Reggio Calabria.

The city of the Riace Bronzes and the Morgana Fairy, where the most beautiful kilometer in Italy depicts the huge and majestic Sicily with the smoldering Etna volcano.

It is one of the most old and distinctive cities in Calabria.

The tour lasts around 3 hours and includes a visit to the archeological museum, which houses the Riace bronzes, as well as a walk through the harbor, Corso Garibaldi, and the Cathedral of Maria S. Assunta.

Ages from 0-120

Duration: 3hours 40m

Start time: Check availability with the phone number provided.

Mobile ticket

Live guide: English and Italian

What is Included:

- ❖ Tourist guide
- ❖ Entry and Admission - Basilica Cattedrale di Reggio Calabria Maria SS Assunta

Archeological Tour in Reggio Calabria

Guided Tour of the Riace Bronzes and the Archaeological Museum of Reggio Calabria

Phone number: +1 855 275 5071

This a classic tour in Reggio Calabria tailored to exploring the Riace Bronzes and the Archaeological Museum of Reggio Calabria.

Ages from 0-120

Duration: 3hours 40m

Start time: Check availability with the phone number provided.

Mobile ticket

Live guide: English and Italian

What is Included:

- ❖ Experience tour guide

Boat Tour in Reggio Calabria

3-Hour Boat Tour of Scilla and Bagnara Caves

Phone number: +1 855 275 5071

Scilla by boat is a slow journey, to explore one of the most beautiful southern Italy, a journey capable of giving you sweet memories. You travel in safety and with experienced crew

Ages from 0-80, 15 per group

Duration: 3hours 40m

Start time: Check availability with the phone number provided.

Mobile ticket

Live guide in Italian

Chapter 8: Rest, Relaxation, and Accommodations in Reggio Calabria

Tips and tricks of Getting the Best Hotels, Accommodation, and Vacation Rentals in Reggio Calabria

Reggio Calabria is a beautiful city recognized for its rich history, spectacular beaches, and breathtaking scenery. When planning your journey to Reggio Calabria, it is critical to select the best hotels, accommodations, and vacation rentals to ensure a comfortable and memorable stay.

In this guide, we will give you helpful tips and tricks to help you make informed decisions and find the best accommodation option for your visit.

1. Research and Plan in Advance:

To make the most of your stay in Reggio Calabria, you should conduct extensive study and plan your trip ahead of time.

Begin by determining your travel dates, reason of visit, and budget. This information will serve as the foundation for your search, allowing you to make smarter decisions.

Consider the time of year you intend to come, as Bergamo has peak tourist seasons throughout the summer months and important events.

2. Choose the Right Location:

Reggio Calabria is recognized for its historical beauty, cobblestone streets, and mediaeval buildings.

Consider your tastes and priorities while choosing a location.

3. Read Reviews and Ratings:

To assess the quality and service provided by hotels, lodgings, and vacation rentals, read reviews and ratings from prior guests.

Websites like Booking.com, and Google Reviews are great places to get comments and insights. Pay attention to recent reviews to ensure the information is current and useful.

Look for consistent, favorable feedback on cleanliness, customer service, and overall experience.

4. Set a Realistic Budget.

Reggio Calabria provides a wide selection of options to meet a variety of budgets. Luxury hotels may offer exclusive amenities and services, but there are also low-cost accommodations and vacation rentals that provide comfort and convenience without breaking the bank.

Prioritize your needs and budget accordingly. Keep in mind that costs fluctuate based on the season, so visit during the shoulder seasons for great deals.

5. Compare Prices and Deals:

To get the greatest bargain, compare prices from multiple sources. Use hotel booking services, travel bureaus, or even make direct reservations through hotel websites.

Keep a look out for special promotions, discounts, and package deals provided by hotels during certain seasons or events. If possible, be flexible about your travel dates, as rates might fluctuate greatly depending on the time of year. To save money, consider bundling your hotel with extra services such as flights or vehicle hire.

6. Consider facilities and Services:

When selecting hotels, prioritize facilities and services that matter to you. Some important features to consider include free Wi-Fi, parking availability, breakfast selections, room size, fitness facilities, and on-site eateries.

Make a list of your priorities and use it as a guideline during your quest. If you have unique requirements, such as accessibility or dietary restrictions, please contact the hotel directly to check that they can accommodate you.

7. Get In Touch.

 If you have specific requirements or preferences, please contact hotels, motels, or vacation rentals directly. Discuss your needs with the team and ask any questions you might have.

This direct communication allows you to judge their responsiveness and readiness to accommodate your needs, resulting in a more personalized experience. They may also provide further information or recommendations for the surrounding area.

8. Consider Vacation Rentals and Alternative Accommodations:

In addition to hotels, look into vacation rentals, apartments, villas, and bed & breakfasts. These solutions typically offer a more immersive and authentic experience, allowing you to live like a local. Websites such as Airbnb and HomeAway provide a diverse selection of holiday rentals to fit a variety of preferences and budgets.

Read the property descriptions attentively, look at the images, and read past guest reviews to guarantee the rental's dependability and quality.

9. Consider Location Convenience:

Look for accommodations near popular attractions, public transportation, and amenities like restaurants, stores, and supermarkets.

This will save you time and effort throughout your stay while also improving your entire experience in Bergamo.

Look for accommodations that are conveniently located near public transportation, since this will allow you to easily explore the city and its environs.

10. Secure your selected dates and accommodation type by booking early and confirming your reservation.

Reggio Calabria is a popular tourist destination, thus supply may be limited, particularly during high seasons. Double-check your reservation information and confirm with the hotel or lodging provider a few days before your arrival to avoid misunderstandings or last-minute problems.

Finding the best hotels, lodgings, and vacation rentals in Reggio Calabria needs careful planning, research, and consideration of multiple criteria.

You may make informed decisions and locate the best hotel option for your needs and budget by doing extensive research, reading reviews, comparing costs, and taking your budget and preferences into account.

Looking into alternate accommodations, such as vacation rentals, can provide a unique and engaging experience.

Following these tips and tricks will ensure that you have a comfortable and happy stay in this beautiful Italian city.

Enjoy your travels!

Hotels in Reggio Calabria

Luxury Hotels in Reggio Calabria

1. Al Castello Luxury B&B

Address: Via Gregorio Palestino, Reggio Calabria, near Aragonese Castle

Phone: +39 338 586 0282

Website: https://alcastello.info/

2. Hotel Medinblu

Address: Via Demetrio Tripepi 98, 89125 Reggio Calabria RC, Italy

Phone: +39 0965 189 0160

Website: https://www.hotelmedinblu.it/

3. High Definition Hotel

Address: Piazza Indipendenza 23, 89121 Reggio Calabria RC, Italy

Phone: +39 0965 332233

Website: https://www.hdhotel.it/

4. Hotel Excelsior

Address: Via Vittorio Veneto 66, 89123 Reggio Calabria RC, Italy

Phone: +39 0965 312300

Website: https://www.excelsiorreggiocalabria.it/

5. Hotel Continental

Address: Via Florio 10, 89123 Reggio Calabria RC, Italy

Phone: +39 0965 812204

Website: https://www.continentalhotelrc.it/

These hotels offer various luxury amenities and are located close to popular tourist attractions in Reggio Calabria.

Family-Friendly Hotels in Reggio Calabria

1. Grand Hotel Excelsior

Address: Via Vittorio Veneto, 66, 89123 Reggio Calabria, Italy

Phone: +39 0965 812100

Website: https://www.grandexcelsior.it/

2. Hotel Lungomare

Address: Viale Genoese Zerbi, 13/b, 89123 Reggio Calabria, Italy

Phone: +39 0965 813398

Website: https://www.hotellungomare.it/

3. Town House Morgana

Address: Via Girolamo Arcovito, 37, 89127 Reggio Calabria, Italy

Phone: +39 0965 813020

Website: http://www.townhousemorgana.com/

4. Possidonea 28 Bed & Breakfast

Address: Via Possidonea, 28, 89125 Reggio Calabria, Italy

Phone: +39 347 084 9188

Website: https://www.possidonea28.com/

5. White Rooms

Address: Via del Torrione, 18, 89123 Reggio Calabria, Italy

Phone: +39 0965 891251

Website: https://www.whiterooms.it/

These hotels offer family-friendly amenities and are conveniently located in Reggio Calabria, providing easy access to local attractions.

Budget-friendly Hotels in Reggio Calabria

1. Hotel Residence Arcobaleno - Budget-Friendly Hotel

Address: Via Vincenzo Comisso, 30, 89124 Reggio Calabria RC, Italy

Phone: +39 0965 556586

Website: www.arcobaleno-hotel.com

2. Hotel Cristal - Budget-Friendly Hotel

Address: Via Marsala, 64, 89125 Reggio Calabria RC, Italy

Phone: +39 0965 20932

Website: www.hotelcristalrc.it

3. Hotel California - Budget-Friendly Hotel

Address: Via Domenico Muratori, 38, 89129 Reggio Calabria RC, Italy

Phone: +39 0965 812345

Website: www.hotelcaliforniarc.it

4. Hotel Residence Al Pescatore - Budget-Friendly Hotel

Address: Via Arghillà, 82, 89134 Reggio Calabria RC, Italy

Phone: +39 0965 199 6616

Website: www.alpescatorehotel.it

5. Hotel Residence Sirio - Budget-Friendly Hotel

Address: Via Sirio, 8, 89129 Reggio Calabria RC, Italy

Phone: +39 0965 081231

Website: www.residence-sirio.it

Chapter 9: Culinary Delights and Restaurants

Foods and Culinary Delight that a Traveler or Tourist to Reggio Calabria Should Try

Reggio Calabria, a beautiful city in Italy, is noted for its rich history, beautiful architecture, and dynamic culinary scene. Exploring the local food is an integral component of any visit to this gorgeous location.

Reggio Calabria provides a diverse culinary experience, ranging from robust traditional cuisine to exquisite desserts and beverages.

In this post, we'll look at foods and culinary delights that every visitor or tourist should sample when visiting Reggio Calabria.

1. Casencelli:

Casoncelli is a typical packed pasta dish that is the pride of Reggio Calabria cuisine. These tiny, handcrafted dumplings are usually filled with a combination of bread crumbs, cheese, and minced pork, seasoned with local herbs like as sage and parsley.

The contents is then neatly tucked into fresh pasta pockets. Casoncelli are topped with melted butter, crisp pancetta, and grated Grana Padano cheese. This dish's tastes and textures complement each other beautifully.

2. Polenta e Osei:

Polenta e Osei is a distinctive and well-known Reggio Calabria dish that translates as "polenta and birds." It is made up of a soft polenta foundation topped with roasted small game birds like thrushes or quails.

The birds are often marinated in red wine and spices before being cooked to perfection. The luscious flesh of the birds, paired with the creamy polenta, provides a harmonic taste profile that is really unique.

3. Stracciatella Gelato.

Enjoy the silky richness of Stracciatella gelato, a famous Italian ice cream flavor from Reggio Calabria. It starts with a creamy vanilla gelato base that's been carefully infused with fine chocolate shavings. Stracciatella is made by dripping melted chocolate into a churning gelato mixture, creating fine flakes that provide a wonderful crunch to each taste.

4. Taleggio Cheese.

Reggio Calabria is known for its delicious cheeses, and Taleggio is a genuine jewel. This semi-soft, washed-rind cheese made from cow's milk has a rich, creamy texture and a somewhat acidic taste. Its unique scent and earthy overtones make it an ideal accent to any cheese platter.

For a true Reggio Calabria experience, pair it with crusty bread, dried fruit, and a glass of local red wine.

5. Polenta Taragna:

Another popular dish in Reggio Calabria is Polenta Taragna. This substantial and cozy recipe blends cornmeal and buckwheat flour, creating a distinct texture and earthy taste.

The inclusion of buckwheat gives the polenta a somewhat nutty flavor and a lovely speckled look. Polenta Taragna is frequently served with savory stews, such as braised meats or wild game, letting the flavors to blend into a pleasant and rustic meal.

6) Torta Donizetti:

Torta Donizetti is a dessert that must be tried. This lovely cake honors Gaetano Donizetti, a well-known composer born in Bergamo. It consists of layers of light sponge cake filled with a delectable blend of chocolate, hazelnut, and cream.

The cake is elegantly adorned with powdered sugar and chocolate shavings. Each mouthful contains a balanced combination of tastes and textures to please any sweet craving.

7. Polenta e Concia:

Polenta e Concia is a simple yet excellent meal that showcases the tastes of Reggio Calabria. It's made of grilled polenta pieces topped with melted local cheeses like Bitto or Casera and sprinkled with aromatic extra virgin olive oil.

The end product is a delicious blend of textures and tastes. The creamy cheese, crunchy polenta shell, and fruity olive oil undertones combine to produce a wonderful flavor symphony.

8. Bergamot liqueur:

Bergamot liquor is made from the fragrant peel of bergamot oranges, this liqueur has a pleasant and zesty flavor.

Bergamot liqueur may be consumed plain, on the rocks, or as a foundation for cocktails, bringing a particular local flavor to your drinking experience.

9. Panettone:

Although Panettone is traditionally linked with Milan, it is equally popular in Reggio Calabria during the Christmas season. This sweet bread loaf, studded with candied fruits and raisins, has a fluffy texture and a delicate taste.

It includes a unique twist, such as the addition of local honey or almonds. It is frequently served with a cup of hot chocolate or spiced wine, resulting in a pleasant and festive pairing that invokes Christmas mood.

10) Scarpinocc:

Scarpinocc is a classic Reggio Calabria pasta dish. These little, twisted ravioli are often filled with a delicious blend of cheese, herbs, and sautéed breadcrumbs.

The filling varies significantly based on the recipe, although it typically contains local cheeses such as Taleggio or Parmigiano-Reggiano.

Scarpinocc are served with melted butter and a sprinkling of sage leaves, creating a delectable combination of textures and flavors. The delicate pasta, delicious filling, and fragrant butter make for a cozy and pleasant dinner.

11) Moscato di Scanzo:

Wine connoisseurs should not pass up the opportunity to try Moscato di Scanzo. This uncommon and coveted red dessert wine is only produced in the adjacent Scanzo area, which is not far from Bergamo.

Moscato di Scanzo is made from Moscato grapes that are let to dry before fermentation. It has a thick and velvety texture with powerful aromas of ripe cherries and traces of spices. It goes well with chocolate-based desserts and aged cheeses, delivering a sweet and sumptuous finale to your dinner.

12. Polenta e Luganega:

Polenta e Luganega is a traditional Reggio Calabria dish that celebrates the region's love of polenta and sausage. Luganega, a native pig sausage, is grilled or cooked in a fragrant tomato sauce and served atop creamy polenta.

The combination of the smoky and delicious sausage with the smooth and cozy polenta provides a delightful and soothing dinner that reflects Reggio Calabria's culinary traditions.

Reggio Calabria's culinary delights reflect its rich cultural past and regional customs. From savory foods like Casoncelli and Polenta e Concia to sweet sweets like Torta Donizetti and Panettone, the city has a wide variety of tastes to satisfy your taste buds.

For a really satisfying gourmet experience, match your meals with local wines and liqueurs such as Moscato di Scanzo and Bergamot liqueur.

Even if you are a foodie or an adventurous visitor, discovering Reggio Calabria's culinary delights is an important part of immersing yourself in the city's culture.

Restaurants in Reggio Calabria

1. Mamas Pellaro

Address: Via Nazionale, 244, 89134 Pellaro RC, Italy

Phone: +39 0965 630 383

2. Adduma Beef Restaurant

Address: Via Vittorio Veneto, 77, 89123 Reggio Calabria RC, Italy

Phone: +39 338 104 0821

3. Officina del Gusto

Address: Via Villini Svizzeri, 33, 89124 Reggio Calabria RC, Italy

Phone: +39 0965 24747

4. Fratelli la Bufala Reggio

Address: Via Zecca, 3/5, 89125 Reggio Calabria RC, Italy

Phone: +39 0965 894116

5. Le Vie del Gusto

Address: Via Demetrio Tripepi, 118, 89125 Reggio Calabria RC, Italy

Phone: +39 0965 24004

6. Timo Restaurant

Address: Via Cattolica dei Greci, 29, 89135 Reggio Calabria RC, Italy

Phone: +39 0965 187 1613

7. Pasqualino Pizza & Vino

Address: Via Filippini, 6, 89125 Reggio Calabria RC, Italy

Phone: +39 0965 020855

8. Villa Campetra Churrascaria

Address: Via Giuseppe De Nava, 128, 89123 Reggio Calabria RC, Italy

Phone: +39 0965 894571

9. Gelato Cesare

Address: Lungomare Falcomatà, 1, 89125 Reggio Calabria RC, Italy

Phone: +39 0965 812 175

10. Ciroma

Address: Via Torrione, 44, 89125 Reggio Calabria RC, Italy

Phone: +39 0965 324 304

These restaurants offer Italian and Mediterranean dishes, ensuring a delightful culinary experience for visitors and tourists

Chapter 10: Tips and Strategies for Having a Memorable Vacation to Reggio Calabria

Reggio Calabria, located in southern Italy, is a mesmerising location noted for its rich history, beautiful coastline, and great local food. Even if you want to sunbathe on lovely beaches or explore historical ruins, Reggio Calabria provides an unforgettable holiday experience.

To make the most of your visit, here are some tips and strategies to help you develop lasting experiences in this wonderful city.

1. Plan ahead and research:

Reggio Calabria has a lot to offer in terms of attractions and activities, so make a plan ahead of time and investigate what interests you the most. Make a list of must-see attractions, such as the National Archaeological Museum and the Riace Bronzes, and research the city's history, culture, and local traditions to gain a better knowledge and respect for the location.

2. Visit the National Archaeological Museum of Reggio Calabria.

Begin your journey of Reggio Calabria by visiting the National Archaeological Museum. This museum displays an amazing collection of artefacts from the city's historical past, including the renowned Riace Bronzes.

These two magnificent bronze sculptures, unearthed in the sea at Riace, are among the most important works of ancient Greek art in the world. Admire the exquisite craftsmanship and learn about its historical importance.

3. Discover the Magnificent Bronzi di Riace.

The Bronzi di Riace (Riace Bronzes) are two renowned Greek sculptures from the fifth century BC. These antique art marvels should not be missed when visiting Reggio Calabria.

Admire their realistic features, exquisite intricacies, and powerful presence. Learn about their intriguing discovery and the ongoing mystery of their origins.

4. Visit the Historical Centre (Centro Storico):

Walk through the small streets of Reggio Calabria's historic center, known as Centro Storico. Immerse yourself in the city's wonderful ambiance by admiring the stunning architecture, small squares, and local businesses.

Don't miss the opportunity to see Reggio Calabria's Cathedral, which is devoted to the city's patron saint, Saint Paul.

5. Try the local cuisine.

Reggio Calabria is well-known for its wonderful food, which reflects the region's rich agricultural history and proximity to the sea.

Try typical foods like 'nduja, a spicy spreadable salami produced from locally obtained Calabrian chilli peppers, and swordfish, a local speciality that is frequently served grilled or in savoury sauces.

 Visit the city's colourful street markets to sample fresh fruits, vegetables, and local cheeses.

For a really genuine gastronomic experience, pair your dishes with a glass of Calabrian wine like Cirò or Greco di Bianco.

6. Take a boat trip to the Aeolian Islands.

Reggio Calabria serves as a gateway to the beautiful Aeolian Islands, a volcanic archipelago off Sicily's northern coast. Take a boat tour from the port of Reggio Calabria to see these gorgeous islands, each with its own distinct personality.

Visit Stromboli to observe its active volcano and enjoy the excitement of a nocturnal walk to see its explosions. Relax on the beautiful beaches of Lipari and Salina, or relax in the hot waters of Vulcano.

The Aeolian Islands provide a wonderful retreat from the mainland and are a must-see vacation.

7. Relax on Beautiful Beaches:

Reggio Calabria has gorgeous beaches along its coastline, offering plenty of possibilities for relaxation and sun-soaked excursions. Spend the day at Scilla, a quaint fishing community noted for its crystal-clear seas and scenic shoreline.

Take a relaxing plunge in the water, soak up the sun, and eat fresh seafood at one of the beachside eateries. Tropea is another magnificent beach location, known for its spectacular cliffs, white sand beaches, and turquoise seas.

 Even if you love sunbathing, swimming, or simply admiring the coastal beauty, these beaches provide a bit of heaven.

8. Hike through Aspromonte National Park:

Nature lovers will find peace at Aspromonte National Park, a huge wilderness region near Reggio Calabria. Lace up your hiking boots and set off on gorgeous routes that lead to beautiful waterfalls, lush woods, and panoramic views.

Explore the park's varied flora and animals, which include rare orchids and the elusive Calabrian wolf. Don't miss the opportunity to climb Monte Consolino, the park's highest summit, for stunning views of the surrounding area. Aspromonte National Park is a nature lover's dream and an ideal refuge for people seeking both peace and adventure.

9. Visit Riace Marina:

A short drive from Reggio Calabria will take you to Riace Marina, a picturesque seaside community famed for its colourful buildings, gorgeous beaches, and tranquil environment. Stroll down the palm-lined promenade and enjoy the gorgeous views of the Ionian Sea.

Enjoy a gelato from one of the local businesses while taking in the relaxed atmosphere. If you're feeling brave, take a boat cruise down the coast to see secret coves and isolated beaches.

Riace Marina provides a calm respite from Reggio Calabria's hectic daily life, allowing you to relax in a serene beach location.

10. Experience the Nightlife:

Reggio Calabria comes alive after dusk with a dynamic nightlife scene. Explore the city's pubs, clubs, and live music venues to feel the energy. Begin your evening with an aperitivo, a pre-dinner drink served with appetisers, at one of the city center's fashionable pubs.

As the night advances, immerse yourself in the vibrant atmosphere of the local taverns, where you may dance to traditional Calabrian music or the current blockbusters. Engaging with the people and enjoying the dynamic nightlife will make your holiday even more exciting.

11. Participate in Local Festivals and Events:

Reggio Calabria's vibrant festivals and events provide a unique opportunity to experience local culture and customs. Check the event calendar and schedule your visit around festivals like the Procession of the Varia di Palmi, a UNESCO-recognized event with ornate floats and religious processions, or the Tarantella Power Festival, which celebrates traditional music and dance. These events highlight the region's rich cultural heritage and offer an unforgettable experience.

12. Interact with the locals:

Connecting with the people is one of the most effective methods to make your Reggio Calabria holiday genuinely unforgettable. Accept their warm welcome, acquire a few basic Italian words, and engage in conversations to gain insight into the local way of living.

Locals are frequently proud of their city and are eager to provide recommendations for hidden treasures, local restaurants, and off-the-beaten-path activities. Interacting with the locals can help you develop a better knowledge of the culture and make important relationships, which will improve your entire experience.

Reggio Calabria provides several options for a pleasant holiday. Reggio Calabria promises to provide unforgettable experiences that will last with you long after your vacation is over, from seeing ancient treasures to feasting in excellent cuisine, resting on gorgeous beaches, and immersing yourself in local culture.

Embrace the allure of this enchanting location and let it leave an unforgettable impact on your heart.

Online and Offline Map Navigation in Reggio Calabria

On-line Maps.

1. Internet Connection:

Make sure you have a reliable internet connection when exploring Reggio Calabria. If you are going from another country, you may consider purchasing a local SIM card or a portable Wi-Fi device to keep connected.

3. **Map Applications:**

There are a number of popular map applications available for smartphones and tablets.

Here are a few choices:

- ❖ Google Maps:

This popular application provides accurate maps, real-time traffic updates, and transportation options.

- ❖ Apple Maps:

If you have an iPhone or iPad, Apple Maps has an easy-to-use interface and integrates with other Apple devices.

- Maps.me:

This application provides detailed offline maps that may be downloaded in advance and used without an internet connection. It's especially beneficial for travelers who wish to save data or do not have access to the internet.

Points of Interest:

Reggio Calabria's places of interest are well-documented on online maps. You can simply find landmarks, attractions, hotels, restaurants, and other places to visit. Tapping on a specific place typically yields extra information such as reviews, contact information, and opening hours.

Satellite View:

Most online map apps have a satellite view, which shows the terrain and landmarks from an aerial viewpoint. This tool can help you better comprehend your surroundings and identify important locations in Bergamo.

Live traffic Updates:

If you're driving, online maps can give real-time traffic updates, allowing you to plan the best routes to avoid traffic and maximize your trip time.

Street View:

Some map applications, such as Google Maps, have a street view option. Street view allows you to visually explore Reggio Calabria's streets at ground level, providing a more realistic experience and helping you become acquainted with that area before to your visit.

Offline Maps.

1. **Downloading Offline Maps:**

Many map apps let you download maps for offline usage.

Here's how to get offline maps, using Google Maps as an example:

- ❖ Open Google Maps and make sure you have a reliable internet connection.
- ❖ Search for " Reggio Calabria" in the search box.

- Once the city is displayed, click the menu (typically three horizontal lines) and pick "Offline Maps" or a similar option.
- Choose "Select Your Own Map" or "Custom Area" and zoom in or out to customize the map area you wish to save.
- Tap "Download" and wait for the offline map to be downloaded and saved on your device.

GPS & Offline Navigation:

With an offline map downloaded, you will use your device's GPS to navigate Reggio Calabria even without an online connection. The map will show your location as a blue dot, allowing you to follow your progress and locate your route.

Points of Interest and Searches:

Offline maps generally contain a search tool to help you identify specific places or areas of interest. Enter the name or address of the location you are searching for, and the map will show it on the downloaded map data.

Offline Directions:

Even while offline, you can use offline maps to get directions between two sites. After you enter your starting location and destination, the app will determine the best route using offline map data. It's worth noting that turn-by-turn navigation may not be available offline, but the map will give you an overview of the route and allow you to follow it visually.

Map Updates.

Keep in mind that offline maps may not always include the most recent information, such as new highways or changes in areas of interest.

To guarantee you have the most up-to-date information, update your offline maps on a regular basis or switch to online maps when you have access to the internet.

Remember to prepare ahead of time, have a backup plan, and keep a paper map on hand in case of technological problems or an emergency. Exploring Reggio Calabria with online and offline maps can help you navigate the city and discover the activities and amenities you want.

Enjoy your stay in Reggio Calabria.

Basic Communication Words to help a Traveler to Reggio Calabria Communicate Easily

1. Hello - Ciao

2. Goodbye - Arrivederci

3. Yes - Sì

4. No - No

5. Please - Per favore

6. Thank you - Grazie

7. Excuse me - Scusa

8. Sorry - Mi dispiace

9. Help - Aiuto

10. I don't understand - Non capisco

11. Do you speak English? - Parli inglese?

12. Where is...? - Dove si trova...?

13. How much does it cost? - Quanto costa?

14. Can you recommend a good restaurant? - Puoi consigliare un buon ristorante?

15. I need a doctor - Ho bisogno di un medico

16. Where is the bathroom? - Dove si trova il bagno?

17. I would like... - Vorrei...

18. Can you help me? - Puoi aiutarmi?

19. I'm lost - Mi sono perso/a

20. I'm sorry, I don't speak Italian - Mi dispiace, non parlo italiano

21. What time is it? - Che ora è?

22. Where can I find a taxi? - Dove posso trovare un taxi?

23. Is there Wi-Fi here? - C'è il Wi-Fi qui?

24. Can you show me on the map? - Puoi mostrarmelo sulla mappa?

25. Is this seat taken? - È occupato questo posto?

26. Can I have the bill, please? - Posso avere il conto, per favore?

27. Can you recommend any local attractions? - Puoi consigliare delle attrazioni locali?

28. I'm vegetarian - Sono vegetariano/a

29. Do you have any vegetarian options? - Avete opzioni vegetariane?

30. Cheers! - Salute!

31. What is your name? - Come ti chiami?

32. Nice to meet you - Piacere di conoscerti

33. Can you repeat that, please? - Puoi ripetere, per favore?

34. Where can I buy tickets? - Dove posso comprare i biglietti?

35. Is there a pharmacy nearby? - C'è una farmacia nelle vicinanze?

36. Can you help me find my hotel? - Puoi aiutarmi a trovare il mio hotel?

37. Is there a bank here? - C'è una banca qui?

38. Is it far from here? - È lontano da qui?

39. What is the weather like today? - Com'è il tempo oggi?

40. Can you recommend a good place to shop? - Puoi consigliare un bel posto per fare shopping?

41. Do you have a menu in English? - Avete un menu in inglese?

42. Can you take a photo of me, please? - Puoi fare una foto di me, per favore?

43. Is there a post office nearby? - C'è un ufficio postale nelle vicinanze?

44. I'm looking for a souvenir - Sto cercando un souvenir

45. Can you speak slowly, please? - Puoi parlare lentamente, per favore?

46. Can you help me with my luggage? - Puoi aiutarmi con i bagagli?

47. Is there a tourist information center? - C'è un centro informazioni turistiche?

48. What is the best way to get to...? - Qual è il modo migliore per arrivare a...?

49. Can you recommend a good hotel? - Puoi consigliare un buon hotel?

50. Have a nice day! - Buona giornata!

These words and phrases should help you navigate through basic communication situations while traveling in Reggio Calabria.

Enjoy your trip!

Detailed Itinerary
A 14-day Itinerary for Reggio Calabria, Italy.

Day 1: Arrival and Introduction.

Morning:

Arrive in Reggio Calabria.

Check in to your accommodation and freshen up.

To become familiar, go for a leisurely walk in the city center.

Afternoon:

Visit the National Archaeological Museum of Reggio Calabria to see the renowned Riace Bronzes.

Evening:

Have a welcome dinner in a typical Calabrian restaurant.

Day 2: Exploring the Historic Centre.

Morning:

Visit the Reggio Calabria Cathedral.

Explore Piazza Italia and its neighboring historic structures.

Afternoon:

Walk down Corso Garibaldi, the major retail street.

Visit the Aragonese Castle.

Evening:

Stroll around the Lungomare Falcomatà, dubbed "the most beautiful kilometer in Italy."

Day 3: Scilla and Chianalea.

Morning:

Take a short excursion to Scilla. Discover the lovely fishing town of Chianalea.

Afternoon:

Visit Ruffo Castle in Scilla and take in the scenery.

Evening:

Return to Reggio Calabria for supper at a beachside restaurant.

Day 4: Pentedattilo.

Morning:

Visit the beautiful town of Pentedattilo.

Visit the ruins and take in the breathtaking views.

Afternoon:

Have lunch at a neighborhood trattoria.

Continue to explore the nearby region.

Evening:

Return to Reggio Calabria and relax in your hotel.

Day 5: Archaeological sites.

Morning:

Explore the ancient Greek city of Locri Epizephyrii.

Afternoon:

Visit the archaeological site and the museum.

Evening:

Return to Reggio Calabria for a leisurely evening.

Day 6: Trip to Gerace.

Morning:

Travel to Gerace, a mediaeval hilltop town.

Visit Norman Castle and Cathedral.

Afternoon:

Explore the small alleyways and have lunch at a nearby eatery.

Evening:

Return to Reggio Calabria and eat at a nearby pizzeria.

Day 7: Beach Day at Lido Comunale

Morning:

Visit Lido Comunale for a relaxing beach day.

Swim across the clear waters of the Tyrrhenian Sea.

Afternoon:

Enjoy seaside food and beverages.

Participate in water sports or simply sunbathe.

Evening:

Enjoy dinner at a beachside restaurant.

Day 8: Cultural immersion.

Morning:

Visit the Pinacoteca Civica to discover local artwork.

Afternoon:

Take a local cooking class to discover traditional Calabrian dishes.

Evening:

Enjoy the dish you created in culinary class.

Day 9: Aspromonte National Park.

Morning:

Take a guided walk of Aspromonte National Park.

Hike to view the stunning waterfalls and various flora and animals.

Afternoon:

Have a picnic lunch at the park.

Evening:

Return to Reggio Calabria and relax in your hotel.

Day 10: Reggio Calabria's Modern Attractions.

Morning:

Visit the Civic Art Gallery.

Afternoon:

Explore the Botanical Gardens.

Evening:

Indulge in a sophisticated Italian supper at a stylish restaurant.

Day 11: Trip to Stilo.

Morning:

Travel to Stilo, the site of the Cattolica di Stilo, a Byzantine church.

Afternoon:

Explore the old town and eat local food during lunch.

Evening:

Return to Reggio Calabria and have a peaceful evening.

Day 12: Culinary delights.

Morning:

Visit a local market and try the fresh products.

Afternoon:

Take a cuisine tour and sample regional specialties.

Evening:

Dine at a popular restaurant recognized for its Calabrian cuisine.

Day 13: Relaxation and Shopping.

Morning:

Spend the morning at a nearby spa to be pampered.

Afternoon:

Along Corso Garibaldi, you may shop for souvenirs and local crafts.

Evening:

Have a goodbye supper in a fancy dining establishment.

Day 14: Departure.

Morning:

Savor a leisurely breakfast.

Pack and prepare for leave.

Afternoon:

Take one last walk down Lungomare Falcomatà.

Evening:

Depart from Reggio Calabria.

Enjoy your visit to Reggio Calabria!

Conclusion

Reggio Calabria provides a compelling vacation experience by combining history, natural beauty, and a rich cultural legacy. This beautiful city, set between the craggy Aspromonte Mountains and the blue waters of the Ionian Sea, has a multitude of attractions that will captivate any traveler.

Reggio Calabria is a treasure trove of historical and natural beauties, from the world-renowned Bronzi di Riace and the ancient Greek statues housed in the National Archaeological Museum to the spectacular panoramic views at the summit of the Aspromonte.

The beautiful beachfront promenade, Lungomare Falcomatà, is ideal for leisurely strolls, while the lively Corso Garibaldi is lined with stores, cafés, and restaurants serving delectable Calabrian cuisine.

Reggio Calabria is an excellent starting point for exploring the region's hidden beauties, like the charming fishing villages of Scilla and Bova, as well as the gorgeous beaches along the Costa Viola.

The inhabitants' friendliness and kindness give an added dimension of appeal to an already captivating region.

Reggio Calabria offers an extraordinary experience for anyone seeking cultural immersion, outdoor excursions, or just relaxing on sun-kissed beaches.

So, pack your bags and travel to this lovely city, where ancient history meets dynamic modern life, to make experiences that will last a lifetime.

Appendix
Map of Reggio Calabria

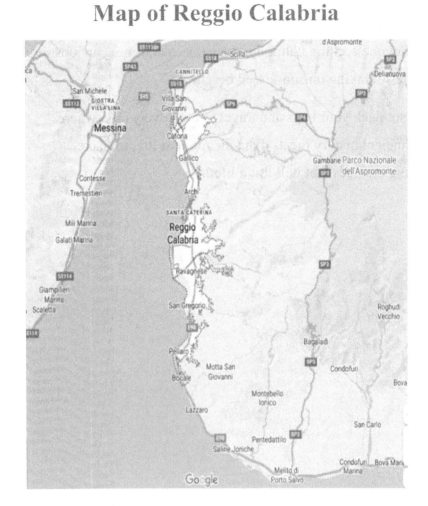

https://maps.app.goo.gl/gva8PzQ4g5zH19qV6

Map of the Top Attractions in Reggio Calabria

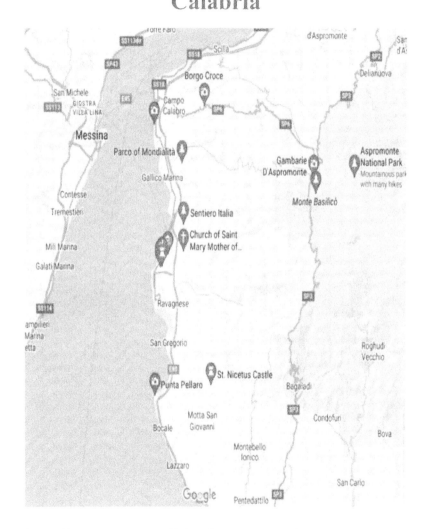

https://maps.app.goo.gl/zhr1fcsaBBP93x7SA

Map of the Beaches in Reggio Calabria

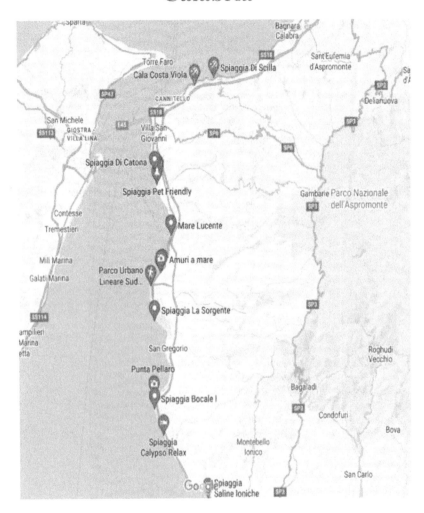

https://maps.app.goo.gl/oN6onV2CEiPednzc6

Map of the Hotels in Reggio Calabria

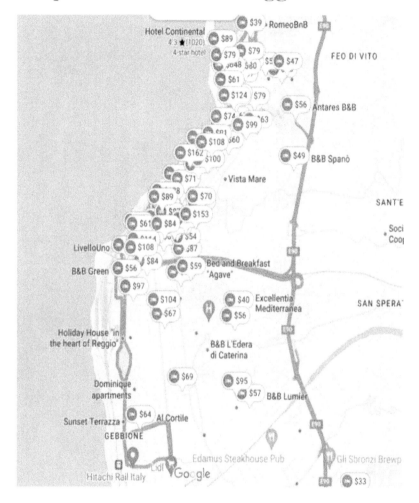

https://maps.app.goo.gl/xJ9bbJKQobS4xP3W8

Map of the Vacation Rentals in Reggio Calabria

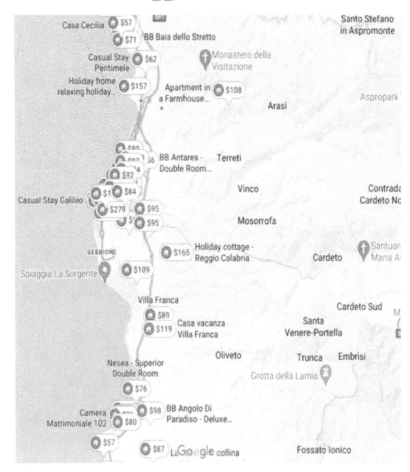

https://maps.app.goo.gl/9rguaT1HE16X1anu6

Map of the Restaurants in Reggio Calabria

https://maps.app.goo.gl/3yQHJqBM9wMWRSVV6

Map of the Markets and Shopping Centers in Reggio Calabria

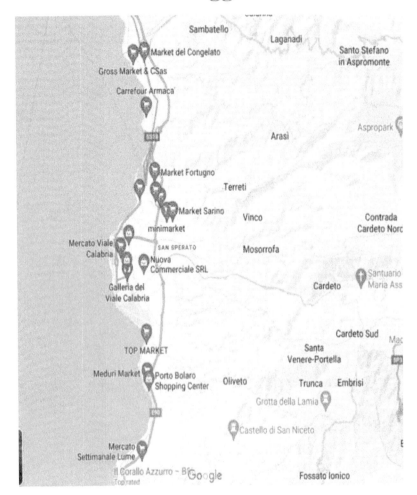

https://maps.app.goo.gl/8dEk3kDDVwmFvTsS9

Image Attributions

https://pixabay.com/photos/scilla-calabria-italy-1185547/ (Book Cover)

https://pixabay.com/photos/san-nicola-arcella-sea-calabria-1979120/ (Book Cover)

Made in the USA
Monee, IL
18 August 2024

64110692R00115